Neil R. Lightfoot

The
Parables
of
Jesus

Volume 2

Revised Edition

THE WAY OF LIFE
SERIES

A·C·U
PRESS
Abilene, Texas

Table of Contents

THE PARABLE OF THE CHIEF SEATS

"Now he told a parable to those who were invited, when he marked how they chose the places of honor, saying to them. 'When you are invited by any one to a marriage feast, do not sit down in a place of honor, lest a more eminent man than you be invited by him; and he who invited you both will come and say to you, "Give place to this man." and then you will begin with shame to take the lowest place. But when you are invited, go and sit in the lowest place, so that when your host comes he may say to you, "Friend, go up higher"; then you will be honored in the presence of all who sit at table with you. For every one who exalts himself will be humbled, and he who humbles himself will be exalted.' "

(Luke 14:7-11)

Lesson 1

"HE WHO HUMBLES HIMSELF"

This parable is a bit of Jesus' table-talk as he ate in the house of a distinguished Pharisee. It was a sabbath meal, and from the beginning the Pharisees had been watching to see what he would do. So he astounded them by healing a man on the sabbath. "Is it not lawful to do good on the sabbath?", he had reasoned.

Long ago, customs observed at dinners were quite different from ours today. It is well-known that the ancients of Greek and Roman times ate their meals in reclining positions on low couches drawn up against low tables. Ordinarily the tables were U-shaped, which allowed the servants to serve food about the table with ease. At the head of the table was placed the honored guest, in Jewish circles this honor always being reserved for the rabbis. On his right and left were placed the next most honored guests, and the others were seated on around the table in descending order of importance. Quite often the exact hour of the meal was not announced. Some guests would arrive early, others would come late. In Jesus' day, many of the Pharisees, especially those of the more prominent sort, would time their arrival so they could make an auspicious entrance and in the presence of all receive the chief seats.

At this particular feast which Jesus attended on the sabbath, the Pharisees were scrutinizing his every move. They were watching him, and He was watching them. He noticed how they came in, slyly maneuvering around the table for the places of honor. So he spoke to them a parable that was a rebuke of their table manners and a warning on their unsafe spiritual condition. "When you are invited to a feast," he said, "don't pick out the best seats. If you do, suppose someone who is a real dignitary comes in. The host will have to ask you to relinquish

1

your seat, and you will be embarrassed to have to go to the foot of the table. If, on the other hand, you at first take a lower seat, the host will urge you to come up higher, and you will be elevated in the sight of all."

This piece of advice that Jesus gave the Pharisees is called a "parable." It is not a parable that tells a story, but it is still a parable because the lesson is to be interpreted figuratively. It is a parable in the true sense of the word, a comparison that teaches on right relationships in the kingdom of God.

Principle of Humility

The concluding statement of the parable is, "For every one who exalts himself will be humbled, and he who humbles himself will be exalted" (Luke 14:11). It was a favorite saying of Jesus, a point he often emphasized (see Matthew 23:12; Luke 18:14). It was a truth often remembered in the early church. It was taught by Paul and James and Peter. "Do nothing from selfishness or conceit, but in humility count others better than yourselves. Let each of you look not only to his own interests, but also to the interests of others" (Philippians 2:3,4). "Humble yourselves before the Lord and he will exalt you" (James 4: 10). "Clothe yourselves, all of you, with humility toward one another, for 'God opposes the proud, but gives grace to the humble.' Humble yourselves therefore under the mighty hand of God, that in due time he may exalt you" (1 Peter 5:5, 6). It stands as a basic law in the Messiah's kingdom that the only way for men to go up is for them to go down.

Pathway to Humility

The principle of humility is obvious and clear. But it is not always easy to find the path that leads to humility. How do we begin? Where is the starting-point of true humility? The place to begin is with oneself. Away from the whirl and rush of things, in quiet, uninterrupted solitude each person needs to submit to the rigor of self-evaluation. And in the lives of all of us there is much that should keep us humble.

1. Our physical and bodily weaknesses should keep us humble. Physically speaking, man is dust.

As a father pities his children,
　　so the Lord pities those who fear him.
For he knows our frame;
　　he remembers that we are dust.
As for man, his days are like grass;
　　he flourishes like a flower of the field;
for the wind passes over it, and it is gone,
　　and its place knows it no more.

Psalms 103:13-16

A man can be an architect or an astronomer, a soldier or a statesman, but no man is as mighty as he would like to be. There are trails where man cannot go, cliffs and mountains that he cannot scale, and galaxies in space which he cannot subdue. Besides this, man lives his days in the midst of suffering and tears. He does not know how to ward off pain. He is unable to defend himself against disease. He cannot disguise the inevitable marks of old age. He cannot bribe away death. The imminence of death alone is sufficient to keep men humble. That an individual's delicate apparatus can get so quickly out of balance, that his bodily systems can be so easily disturbed, that his house of clay can be so swiftly swept away — all of these things show how insecure life is and when remembered will dash to pieces our selfish pride.

2. Our mental limitations should keep us humble. For centuries man has been accumulating facts and perfecting methods. If all of this knowledge could be put together in one storehouse, it would still be infinitesimally small as compared with what man does not know. Advancements in technology and scientific break-throughs come painfully slow. No one is more keenly aware of this than the scholar. The real scholar is perpetually shamed by his ignorance. In all the history of the world there has not been a truly wise man who was impressed with his wisdom. The learned Socrates was by no means the best-loved citizen of ancient Athens. He had a heartless way about him that delighted in humiliating other people. His favorite pastime was to go through the streets of the city looking for a wise man. When he found a likely candidate, he would corner him, drill him with a series of unanswerable questions, and then leave him in the oblivion of his ignorance. If Socrates was the wisest man in Athens, it was only for the reason, he said, that

he alone knew that he knew nothing at all. Will Rogers put it like this: "We are all ignorant; we're just ignorant of different things." A man may be able to speak ten languages and be wholly unable to keep up his bank balance. A man may be an international authority on the literary classics and not be able to drive a car. A man may be an expert on machines and all sorts of electrical devices and scarcely be able to spell a three-syllable word. The simple truth is that life has grown to such proportions that no one is able to be a master of all the arts and a master of all the sciences. The littleness of our knowledge ought to keep us forever humble.

3. Our moral weaknesses and failures should keep us humble. Carlyle once said: "It is in general more profitable to reckon up our defects than to boast of our attainments."[1] Nowhere are defects more obvious to us than in our moral conduct. The purest and noblest of men are ever conscious of sin. The Apostle Paul is an outstanding example of this. At work in his life was a destructive force of self-contradiction. At times he did not do what he wanted, but he did the very things that he hated. "So," he said, "I find it to be a law that when I want to do right, evil lies close at hand. Wretched man that I am! Who will deliver me from this body of death?" (Romans 7:21,24). It is the same apostle who speaks of himself as the chiefest of sinners (see 1 Timothy 1:15). Francis of Assisi, who spent his life in service of the poor, points to himself and says: "Nowhere is there a more wretched, a more miserable, a poorer creature than I." Honest self-examination will bring us face to face with ourselves so that we can see how little we really are. How many of us would be willing right now to meet God in judgment on the terms of our innate goodness and on the basis of the works which we have done in his name? The sum total of our kindness, of our generosity and of our good deeds is deplorably small. This above all things, the mediocre goodness that is in the best of us, should make us conscious of the necessity of humility.

Pattern of Humility

When a man meets Jesus Christ and puts his life beside that Life, the marked difference brings guilt and grief. On that last

---

[1]Carlyle, "Signs of the Times," Essays.

night, within the shadow of the cross, a quarrel arose among his disciples as to which of them was the greatest (Luke 22:24-27). We do not know how the argument began. But since Jesus had gathered with his group to eat the Passover meal, the most important Jewish observance of the year, it is quite likely that the strife was over the seating arrangements around the table. What a poignant tragedy that Jesus in these last hours had to witness his own disciples, like the Pharisees, scrambling for seats of distinction. To put an end to the dispute, Jesus asked: "For which is the greater, one who sits at table, or one who serves? Is it not the one who sits at table? But I am among you as one who serves" (vs. 27). Then Jesus arose from his place, stripped off his garments, girded himself with a towel, as a slave would do, and one by one washed his disciples' feet (see John 13:3ff.). They sat there dumbfounded, utterly disgraced, not believing that they could have acted so selfishly. It was scarcely necessary that Jesus remind them to do as he had done. The Prince of Glory bathing their feet! It was a lesson of love and service that they could not forget.

People in the day of Christ did not believe that a man who pushes himself will be abased, nor that a man who lowers himself will in the end be victorious. And few people believe it today. But Jesus taught the contrary, and what he taught he practiced. When he came into the world he slept in a manger and when he died he reclined on a cross. Neither at his birth nor at his death could he find a more lowly place. The contrast of his life with our lives is to our shame.

Discussion

1. What is a parable? The Parable of the Chief Seats does not tell a story. In what sense is it a parable?

2. Give the background and the occasion of this parable. Tell something about the eating customs and the seating arrangements in homes during Greek and Roman times.

3. Read the following Scriptures: Matthew 23:12; Luke 18:14; Philippians 2:3,4; James 4:10; 1 Peter 5:5,6. Also read Luke 22:24-27 and John 13:1-17. Discuss these passages in which the principle of humility is emphasized.

4. What is the beginning point of humility? List some of the things that should serve to keep us humble.

5. The Pharisees loved the chief seats (Matthew 23:6; Mark 12:39). What are some things in our lives that parallel their desire for the chief seats?

6. Define humility. Can one become proud of his humility?

THE PARABLE OF THE GREAT SUPPER

"When one of those who sat at table with him heard this, he said to him, 'Blessed is he who shall eat bread in the kingdom of God!' But he said to him, 'A man once gave a great banquet, and invited many; and at the time for the banquet he sent his servant to say to those who had been invited, "Come; for all is now ready." But they all alike began to make excuses. The first said to him, "I have bought a field, and I must go out and see it; I pray you, have me excused." And another said, "I have bought five yoke of oxen, and I go to examine them; I pray you, have me excused." And another said, "I have married a wife, and therefore I cannot come." So the servant came and reported this to his master. Then the householder in anger said to his servant, "Go out quickly to the streets and lanes of the city, and bring in the poor and maimed and blind and lame." And the servant said, "Sir, what you commanded has been done, and still there is room." And the master said to the servant, "Go out to the highways and hedges, and compel people to come in, that my house may be filled. For, I tell you, none of those men who were invited shall taste my banquet." ' "

(Luke 14:15-24)

7

THE PARABLES OF THE MARRIAGE OF THE KING'S SON AND THE WEDDING GARMENT

"And again Jesus spoke to them in parables, saying, 'The kingdom of heaven may be compared to a king who gave a marriage feast for his son, and sent his servants to call those who were invited to the marriage feast; but they would not come. Again he sent other servants, saying, "Tell those who are invited, Behold, I have made ready my dinner, my oxen and my fat calves are killed, and everything is ready; come to the marriage feast." But they made light of it and went off, one to his farm, another to his business, while the rest seized his servants, treated them shamefully, and killed them. The king was angry, and he sent his troops and destroyed those murderers and burned their city. Then he said to his servants, "The wedding is ready, but those invited were not worthy. Go therefore to the thoroughfares, and invite to the marriage feast as many as you find." And those servants went out into the streets and gathered all whom they found, both bad and good; so the wedding hall was filled with guests.

" 'But when the king came in to look at the guests, he saw there a man who had no wedding garment; and he said to him, "Friend how did you get in here without a wedding garment?" And he was speechless. Then the king said to the attendants, "Bind him hand and foot, and cast him into the outer darkness; there men will weep and gnash their teeth." For many are called, but few are chosen.' "

(Matthew 22:1-14)

Lesson 2

THE BANQUET OF THE KINGDOM

The one great quality that dominated the life of Jesus was unselfishness. While he was dining in the presence of the Pharisees, Jesus' thoughts turned to the many people who were not invited. So he spoke to his host in the plainest of terms and said: "When you give a dinner or a banquet, do not invite your friends or your brothers or your kinsmen or rich neighbors, lest they also invite you in return, and you be repaid. But when you give a feast, invite the poor, the maimed, the lame, the blind, and you will be blessed, because they cannot repay you. You will be repaid at the resurrection of the just" (Luke 14:12-14). These were hard words; they were condemning words. His host must have glared at him with eyes of censure and anger. But Jesus, with no further word of explanation, stood his ground. Then, in an effort to break the spell and dismiss the question, one of the guests exclaimed: "Blessed is he who shall eat bread in the kingdom of God." Jesus responded with a parable that compares his kingdom to a banquet furnished by God.

Parable of the Great Supper

Once a man gave a great banquet. First, in keeping with Oriental customs, a general announcement was sent out to inform everybody of the coming event. The date was specified, but the exact hour was not. On the stated day, when all the preparations had been made and everything was in order, the man sent out his servant to tell his invited friends that the hour had arrived for the supper. But each man, for one reason or another, began to beg off and would not come. The servant returned and reported this to his master. The master burned with anger. If his friends were not going to come, they should

9

have declined at the first invitation and not have waited until the last moment. What was to be done? "Go into town," said the master, "and bring in the bystanders, the poor, the crippled, and the neglected, and let them fill the empty places." The servant obeyed, but still there was room left. " Then hurry out and get those in the country," the master demanded, "for I want the house filled with guests to eat my supper."

Similar Parable

Matthew records a similar parable (see Matthew 22:1-14), so much like this one that interpreters have maintained that they are but two variations of one original story. But the details of the parables, and their backgrounds, are quite different. The one in Matthew follows in close succession the Parable of the Wicked Husbandmen and sounds a warning note to the Jews who would reject their Messiah. The parable in Luke, however, is not as severe in tone, yet it stands as a warning to all men that they should not take the kingdom for granted. The two parables, then, are independent of each other. Their obvious similarities are due to their common source of origin, the Galilean Teacher.

Divine Banquet

The first truth that strikes us here is that Jesus compared his kingdom to a sumptuous banquet. It is significant that most of Luke 14 (vss. 1-25) has to do with feasts and banquets. In this atmosphere Jesus relates a story to show that entering God's kingdom is like coming to a feast. It was the common belief at that time that when the Messiah came, in the golden age of his reign, all of the Jews would be invited in to sit down at the Messiah's table. Jesus made use of this popular notion and taught that the kingdom is like a banquet. The kingdom is not like a long, dreary funeral procession. It is a festive occasion of warm fellowship and unheard of delight. Each follower of Christ in the kingdom, of course, must bear his own burden, each must carry his own cross. But Christ makes it clear that he did not come to darken an already gloomy world. His mission was to bring "the good news" of the kingdom of God.

Since that time, however, this message of Christ has been distorted beyond the point of recognition. Multitudes have come to believe that one cannot enjoy himself if he is a Christian, that to be a Christian is to denounce every joy and pleasure that abound in a beautiful world. Much of this misconception of Christianity arises out of a distorted view of Jesus. The man from Nazareth was indeed the fulfillment of the Old Testament "man of sorrows," the divine servant who "was wounded for our transgressions" and "bruised for our iniquities" (Isa. 53:3-5). But this picture of Jesus as the Suffering Servant has been magnified out of proportion. An example of this is a spurious letter written by a certain Publius Lentulus, a supposed contemporary of Pilate. The letter, which was written in Latin and was composed no earlier than the fourth century A.D., purports to give an actual physical description of Jesus. It reads in part: "In reproof and rebuke he is formidable; in exhortation and teaching, gentle and amiable. He has never been seen to laugh, but oftentimes to weep. His person is tall and erect; his hands and limbs beautiful and straight. In speaking he is deliberate and grave, and little given to loquacity. In beauty he surpasses the children of men."[1] So goes the imaginary description. Yet because it was the first written description of Jesus, it had a lasting effect on the art and sculpture of succeeding ages, so that even today Jesus is often pictured as the man who never laughed. But this is not a picture of Jesus at all. The Jesus of the Gospels was real, of flesh and bone, as human as he was divine. He was not an ascetic, he was not a recluse (see Matthew 11:18, 19). He could not have been the companion of children and the friend of tax-collectors if he was a man who never laughed. On the contrary, some of his expressions, such as a man with a board in his eye (Matthew 7:3-5), indicate that he had a rich sense of humor; and his many parabolic illustrations show that he could enjoy a story as much as any man.

If Jesus lived in a way as to enjoy life, his disciples should do the same. They are not expected, in monk fashion, to withdraw from the world and heap punishments and miseries upon their bodies. Nor are they to be bound, like some of the Puritans of the past, by a code so strict that even toys for children are condemned as "the works of the flesh." John Wesley was a great man, but he made some tragic mistakes concerning children. In the year of 1748, he established a school known as the Kings-

---

[1]As cited by Philip Schaff, *History of the Christian Church*, I, 168-69.

wood School. The children in the school were required to get up at 4 a.m., winter and summer. There were no recess periods, no holidays, and no play of any sort on any day.[2] In contrast to this austerity, Jesus said that his kingdom is a kingdom of joy. It is not a joy of bodily dissipation and sensual living; rather it is a spiritual and eternal and heavenly joy. The joys of God's favor, the redemption from sin, the comfort of the Holy Spirit, the fellowship of the saints, and the peace of God that surpasses understanding — these are the joys of the Christian that make each day like a feast day.

Frivolous Excuses

When the preparations had been made for the banquet and the servant went out to announce its exact hour, the invited guests "all alike began to make excuses." The word "alike" is a translation of an obscure Greek expression *apo mias*. It is usually taken to mean "alike" or "unanimously": thus one and all, as if by previous design, began to decline the invitation. There is a possibility, however, as evidenced by recent information from the papyri discoveries, that the expression *apo mias* means "at once": thus all, without the blink of an eye, immediately began to excuse themselves.[3] Understood either way, it is plain that those invited simply did not want to come.

The excuses that were offered by the intended guests teach certain lessons. The three excuses may be divided into two classes: the first two have to do with earthly possessions and the third concerns earthly ties.

1. *Earthly possessions.* The first man said, "I have bought a field, and I must go out and see it." The second man said, "I have bought five yoke of oxen, and I go to examine them." There is little difference between the excuses. Both men were absorbed in their own interests; both were so tied up in their business affairs that they had time for nothing else. They had too much to do. They could not come. Many people are like that today. The life that now is gets their first attention. Their busi-

---

[2]Robert Southey, *The Life of John Wesley* (New York: Frederick A. Stokes Co., 1903), pp. 225-26.
[3]See Arndt-Gingrich, *A Greek-English Lexicon of the New Testament and Other Early Christian Literature.* 2nd ed. p. 88.

ness is their Bible and "making a living" is their creed. They never seem to have time for other people and, of course, they never have time to worship or pray or think about the future life. Surely this is one reason why God in his wisdom has provided Christians with a special occasion and a special service of worship on the Lord's Day. That day is a special call to put aside the concerns of the week and give attention to the concerns of God. In the assembly brother meets with brother; each encourages the other not to stumble; and each as he reflects on the sacrifice of Christ is reminded once again of the cost of sin. We are exhorted, therefore, not to forsake the worship assembly (Hebrews 10:25). It is not possible for man to live by bread alone (see Matthew 4:4). So we must be sure that the demands of business and earthly possessions do not usurp the demands of God.

2. *Earthly ties.* The third man said, "I have married a wife, and therefore I cannot come." One of the beautiful laws of the Old Testament made allowances for a newly-married man: "When a man is newly married, he shall not go out with the army or be charged with any business; he shall be free at home one year, to be happy with his wife whom he has taken" (Deuteronomy 24:5). Perhaps on the basis of this law the man refused to come. At any rate he felt that he had a perfectly good excuse. He placed the obligations of his family and of his home first, and he expected that everybody would understand.

It is a paradox that something as lovely and sweet as home can stand between a man and his God. Scripture indeed says, "Therefore a man leaves his father and his mother and cleaves to his wife, and they become one flesh" (Genesis 2:24). But to leave father and mother does not mean that one should leave his Father in heaven. Our homes, of course, are among our greatest blessings. But many a great blessing has turned into disaster. There are at least two ways in which we can use our homes wrongfully. First, our home and family ties can occupy the chief spot in our hearts. The excuse of the man who could not leave his wife should be compared with Jesus' statement a few verses later: "If any one comes to me and does not hate his own father and mother and wife and children and brothers and sisters, yes, and even his own life, he cannot be my disciple" (Luke 14:26). Jesus demands an exclusive affection. He wants the whole heart, brother or mother or wife not excepted. Second, our homes can be used selfishly. We can come home after work each day and want to do nothing but relax and enjoy ourselves. Or we can spend so much time and effort making our homes livable that we wrap ourselves up in luxury and shut others out. Regardless of how our homes are built, the windows should always look out on the needs of others. Hospitality was a great virtue in New Testament times (see Romans 12:13; Hebrews 13:2); and hospitality remains today the great glory of a Christian home.

Universal Invitation

The flimsy excuses made the host angry: those especially invited did not want to come. So he sent his servant out into the city to bring in the poor and the maimed and blind and lame. They were gathered from the "streets and lanes" of the town, the public places where those who had no comfortable homes were likely to be found. Still there was room. "Then, go out of the city to the highways and hedgerows," said the host. "I want my house to be full." The immediate application of this points to the Jews. They had rejected Jesus and would not sit at the Messiah's table; therefore, the lower classes of people, publicans, sinners, and even the heathen, would take their places at the royal table. Yet it is a wonderful truth of general application that God wants his house to be full, that He is abundant in mercy and desires the salvation of all. When once his invitation is refused, he returns again and goes to others in order that some will feast at his banquet. The Great Commission is worldwide. The Gospel is for all. The love of God desires a multitude of guests.

What a sight that was when the cripples and downcasts entered the banquet hall — the poor with their heads bowed, the lame leaning on their crutches, the blind groping around for a place to sit. But it was a happy group and a happy occasion. And what of those who did not come? They had closed themselves out. They had sent different excuses, yet there was only one reason why they did not come. They loved other things too much. They refused a generous host. They rejected grace.

Discussion

1. Read the parables of the Marriage of the King's Son and the Wedding Garment (Matthew 22:1-14). Compare and contrast these parables with the Parable of the Great Supper.

2. What lessons are to be drawn from the fact that Jesus compared his kingdom to a banquet?

3. Discuss the nature of the three excuses that were offered. Are the things mentioned in the excuses wrong in themselves? How do our excuses today compare with the excuses given by the invited guests?

4. Give the significance of the statement: "Go out of the city to the highways and hedgerows. I want my house to be full."

5. Is your congregation just taking care of the "good" people or is it relating itself to community problems and needs?

THE PARABLE OF THE TOWER

"For which of you, desiring to build a tower, does not first sit down and count the cost, whether he has enough to complete it? Otherwise, when he has laid a foundation, and is not able to finish, all who see it begin to mock him, saying, 'This man began to build, and was not able to finish.' "

(Luke 14:28-30)

THE PARABLE OF THE KING

"Or what king, going to encounter another king in war, will not sit down first and take counsel whether he is able with ten thousand to meet him who comes against him with twenty thousand? And if not, while the other is yet a great way off, he sends an embassy and asks terms of peace. So therefore, whoever of you does not renounce all that he has cannot be my disciple."

(Luke 14:31-33)

Lesson 3

COUNTING THE COST

The mark of a great leader is to state clearly the conditions that must be met by those who follow him. Jesus of Galilee was that kind of leader. Great multitudes had been following him; many people were excited about him. Some thought that as Messiah he would drive out the Roman horde. Others were fascinated by his strange teachings and his mighty works. Others were just curious. To this motley crowd that was turning the whole affair into a playful extravaganza, Jesus said: "If anyone comes to me and does not hate his own father and mother and wife and children and brothers and sisters, yes, and even his own life, he cannot be my disciple. Whoever does not bear his own cross and come after me, cannot be my disciple" (Luke 14:26-27). Crowding along behind him did not mean discipleship, and Jesus with his stern language makes this unmistakably clear.

To further explain what he meant he chose two illustrations. The first illustration is that of a man who wanted to build a tower. The tower was most likely a vineyard tower (see Matthew 21:33). Quite often in a well-kept vineyard a tower was built to guard against those who might strip the vineyard in harvest time. Before a man began to build a tower, would he not sit down and figure out exactly what it was going to cost? Otherwise, when he began to build and could not finish, he would become a laughing-stock to all who saw him. Jesus as a carpenter had undoubtedly seen a number of men who began to build but ran out of funds before the job was completed. The other illustration is that of a king who contemplated war. Before engaging in a conflict, he calculates the odds and the risks involved. Is he able to stand against twenty thousand with his ten thousand? Are his own soldiers well-trained and eager for battle? Can he advantage himself somehow with the element of surprise? If he cannot afford to do battle, he must send a delegation and ask for peace.

The Hatred Jesus Demands

Before looking at these twin parables more closely, it is necessary to explore at greater length the kind of hatred Jesus demands. An easy and almost universal explanation is that Jesus did not intend for his words to be taken literally, that in reality he did not mean "hate" but rather "love less." But this interpretation, along with many similar interpretations of his strong statements, runs the risk of dulling the sharp edge of Jesus' command. What did Jesus mean when he said that we must hate our fathers and mothers and brothers and sisters? Concerning this paradox of hating others, several points should be noticed.

1. The whole spirit of Jesus' teachings made it impossible that his disciples understand these words in their most literal meaning. Jesus did not seek to crush the tender relationships of human friendships and love. Far from hating their friends, he called on his followers to love even their enemies (see Matthew 5:43-48). He taught them that they must honor their parents and condemned the Pharisaic traditions that by-passed this solemn duty (see Mark 7:9-13). He himself when on the cross committed the care of his mother to a trusted friend (see John 19:26, 27). He spoke against anger and hatred of one's brother and said that it was a kind of murder (see Matthew 5:21-26). Little children he gathered in his arms and blessed (Mark 10:13-16). His teachings and the warm context of his entire life made it quite clear that men were to be loved.

2. The word "hate" is not to be taken to mean that we are to love our relatives and friends with a diminished love. This would be opposed to the heart and soul of Christianity. Husbands are told to love their wives even as Christ loved the church (see Ephesians 5:25). Christians are expected to cultivate "a sincere love of the brethren," and "to love one another earnestly from the heart" (1 Peter 1:22). It is true that we may love the Lord too little; but we cannot love any human being too much. And we shall never love the Lord more by loving our human friends less.

3. The words "hate his own life also" supply the key to the problem. A disciple is to hate his relatives and friends in the same sense that he hates himself. In what sense is a man to hate himself? He must hate whatever in himself is low and base, all that is greedy and selfish, anything that would drag him away from Christ and rob his real self of true values. In the same way he is to hate his relatives and friends. He ought to love them as he loves himself, and he ought to hate them as he hates himself. Whatever in them is pure and right he is to love; whatever is unclean and self-indulgent he is to hate. And if a man's friends come to stand between him and his Lord, if a choice has to be made between natural affection and devotion to Christ, then true disciples must be ready to treat their dearest friends as hated enemies.

Challenge of Christ

If Jesus' stern conditions of discipleship are regarded as determents to superficial enthusiasm, they may also be regarded as challenges to those whose ambition is to live an active and vigorous life. Jesus was uncompromisingly honest. He did not, like most recruiting-officers, keep back the difficult and dangerous in order to enlist men in his service. He wanted no one to come after him under false illusions. Men would have to face up to the task or not follow him at all.

So Jesus taught that men must count the cost if they wish to be his disciples. This is the lesson of the parables on the rash builder and the rash king. A man would be foolish to build a tower without estimating the cost; and a king would be foolish to go to war without taking into consideration the necessary risks. A man who desires to follow Christ must likewise see beforehand the hard and painful struggle that awaits him, and be ready to make the sacrifices required no matter what the cost. Before he begins the Christian life, a man should ask himself several questions.

1. *Am I willing to deny myself?* When a man starts out on the Christian way, it is the end of self. Self-denial is the first condition of discipleship. "If any man wants to come after me," Jesus said, "let him deny himself...." (Matthew 16:24). By this Jesus did not mean a temporary denial of self, a sacrifice of certain pleasures for a week or two in order that some good cause might

be supported. To deny oneself is to live no longer to please the self. The Apostle Paul wrote that he had been crucified with Christ (see Galatians 2:20). He had killed self. He had nailed his passions and lusts to the cross. This is what he told the Colossian Christians that they must do (Colossians 3:5ff.). This is precisely what all men must do who sincerely seek him. And it is a bitter treatment that is required. No death is easy. C. S. Lewis in his inimitable fashion has expressed it like this: "The Christian way is different .... Christ says, 'Give me all. I don't want so much of your time and so much of your money and so much of your work: I want you. I have not come to torment your natural self, but to kill it. No half-measures are any good. I don't want to cut off a branch here and a branch there, I want to have the whole tree down. I don't want to drill the tooth, or crown it, or stop it, but to have it out. Hand over the whole natural self, all the desires which you think innocent as well as the ones you think wicked — the whole outfit. I will give you a new self instead. In fact, I will give you myself: my own will shall become yours.' "[1] That is what Jesus requires. To deny self is in every moment and in every way to say no to self and yes to Jesus Christ.

2. *Am I willing to abide by his teachings?* Before starting out on the Christian way, a man should ask if he is willing to live by Jesus' teachings. Along with this one needs to make sure that his mind is settled as to the claims of Jesus. The Galilean, after all, made extraordinary claims. He was born to be a king (Matthew 2:2) and he told Pilate that he was a king (John 18:36). He professed to be the Christ, the Messiah foretold in the Old Testament (Mark 14:61, 62; John 4:25,26). He said that he was the world's light (John 8:12); the one who could supply living water (John 4:10); the Bread of Life (John 6:35); the Way, the Truth and the Life (John 14:6). In short, he claimed to be the Savior of the world. These were preposterous claims even in that age. Any man would do well to review these claims once again and in this current age of doubt be convinced deep down in his heart that these claims are unequivocally true.

Commitment to Jesus' claims, however, involves living by his teachings. True discipleship means continuing in the words

---

[1]C. S. Lewis, *Mere Christianity* (London: Fontana Books, 1955), pp. 163-64.

of Christ (John 8:31). This is a vital part of the cost that must be counted. It is as though Jesus says to multitudes of his would-be followers: "You say you want to follow me, but are you willing to do what I say? Are you willing to be guided solely by my teachings? Instead of an eye for an eye and a tooth for a tooth, are you prepared to turn the other cheek or go the second mile? Will you love those who hate you? When men persecute you, will you pray for them? Are you ready to exchange earthly treasures for heavenly treasures? Without reservations or any strings attached, are you really willing to put my kingdom first?" These are some of the awesome questions that Christ asks every man. They are questions that sift the multitudes. They are questions that try men's souls. The blueprint of the Christian life is laid out in microcosm in the Sermon on the Mount. Before a man calls himself a disciple, he must come to a definite and affirmative decision about that blueprint.

3. *Am I willing to follow him to the end?* There are many people who are eager to follow Jesus as long as the way is easy and pleasant; but when the going gets hard and the road stretches long, they give it all up. The parable of the tower presents this as a distinct possibility for every Christian. Many Christians, like the reckless builder, start out with a spurt but never finish. They make their big mistake in thinking that the Christian race is only a short distance. But life's race is not a quick, snappy sprint. It is a marathon race, and there is danger present even on the last lap. Bunyan in his *Pilgrim's Progress* tells of one man who successfully completed the hazardous journey upward and then was turned away from the Celestial City.[2] This to Bunyan was a sign that there was a way to hell even from the gates of heaven. The Christian way lasts until the journey's end, and not until a man comes to know something of the toil and the length of that road has he fully counted the cost.

Facing Facts

In every department of life it is good to be honest with oneself and face the facts. If a man wants to devote his life to others in the practice of medicine, there are many pleasures which are

---

[2]John Bunyan, *The Pilgrim's Progress,* ed. Louis L. Martz (New York: Rinehart and Co., 1949), p. 168.

routine to others that he will have to forego. If he does not make allowances for this ahead of time, he will prove to be an eminently unhappy and unsuccessful doctor. If a man wishes to become a scholar, he must first realize that the road is tough, that it requires rigorous self-discipline and years of study alone in the night. A young man may have his heart set on becoming an athlete, he may envision numerous laurels of victory; but unless he is willing to pay the price for excellence, no honors will ever be accorded him. Jesus in these parables does not intend to dampen enthusiasm, but he is saying that the hard facts of the Christian way must be faced or else red-hot enthusiasm will end up in cold despair. Nor does he mean in these parables that it is better not to begin than to begin and fail. He does mean, however, that it is better not to begin, than to begin with a flourish of trumpets and a look of glamour that invites disaster. There is no challenge that compares to the Christian life, and no thrill that exceeds the thrill of the Christian way, but dying with him and taking up his cross is not easy. We must forsake all, and most of all we must forsake ourselves.

Discussion

1. What "hard saying" does Jesus make prior to his speaking the parables of the Tower and the King. List several possible interpretations for this saying. What does it mean in your opinion?

2. What is the main lesson of the parables of the Tower and the King? Do you think that we have neglected to give due attention to these parables?

3. What are some of the questions an individual should ask himself before becoming a Christian? What are some questions that an individual should ask himself after becoming a Christian?

4. Read and discuss selected passages on the principle of self-denial. It has been said that Christians today scarcely practice sacrifice. What do you think? Is there a difference between sacrifice and self-denial?

5. Bunyan learned that there is a way to hell even near the gates of heaven. What lessons are we to gain from this?

6. What is "total commitment"?

THE PARABLE OF THE LOST SHEEP

"Now the tax collectors and sinners were all drawing near to him. And the Pharisees and the scribes murmured, saying, 'This man receives sinners and eats with them.'

"So he told them this parable: 'What man of you, having a hundred sheep, if he has lost one of them, does not leave the ninety-nine in the wilderness and go after the one which is lost, until he finds it? And when he has found it, he lays it on his shoulders, rejoicing. And when he comes home, he calls together his friends and his neighbors, saying to them, "Rejoice with me, for I have found my sheep which was lost." Even so, I tell you, there will be more joy in heaven over one sinner who repents than over ninety-nine righteous persons who need no repentance.' "

(Luke 15:1-7)
(Parallel Passage: Matthew 18:12-14)

THE PARABLE OF THE LOST COIN

" 'Or what woman, having ten silver coins, if she loses one coin, does not light a lamp and sweep the house and seek diligently until she finds it? And when she has found it, she calls together her friends and neighbors, saying, "Rejoice with me, for I have found the coin which I had lost." Even so, I tell you, there is joy before the angels of God over one sinner who repents.' "

(Luke 15:8-10)

"And he said, 'There was a man who had two sons; and the younger of them said to his father, "Father, give me the share of property that falls to me." And he divided his living between them. Not many days later, the younger son gathered all he had and took his journey into a far country, and there he squandered his property in loose living. And when he had spent everything, a great famine arose in that country, and he began to be in want. So he went and joined himself to one of the citizens of that country, who sent him into his fields to feed swine. And he would gladly have fed on the pods that the swine ate, and no one gave him anything. But when he came to himself he said, "How many of my father's hired servants have bread enough and to spare, but I perish here with hunger! I will arise and go to my father and I will say to him. 'Father, I have sinned against heaven and before you; I am no longer worthy to be called your son; treat me as one of your hired servants.' ' And he arose and came to his father. But while he was yet at a distance, his father saw him and had compassion, and ran and embraced him and kissed him. And the son said to him, "Father, I have sinned against heaven and before you; I am no longer worthy to be called your son." But the father said to his servants, "Bring quickly the best robe, and put it on him; and put a ring on his hand, and shoes on his feet; and bring the fatted calf and kill it, and let us eat and make merry; for this my son was dead, and is alive again; he was lost, and is found." And they began to make merry.

" 'Now his elder son was in the field; and as he came and drew near the house, he heard music and dancing. And he said to him, "Your brother has come, and your father has killed the fatted calf, because he has received him safe and sound." But he was angry and refused to go in. His father came out and entreated him, but he answered his father, "Lo, these many years I have served you, and I never disobeyed your command; yet you never gave me a kid, that I might make merry with my friends. But when this son of yours came, who has devoured your living with harlots, you killed for him the fatted calf!" And he said to him, "Son, you are always with me, and all that is mine is yours. It was fitting to make merry and be glad, for this your brother was dead, and is alive; he was lost, and is found." ' "

(Luke 15:11-32)

Lesson 4

"THIS MAN RECEIVES SINNERS"

The fifteenth chapter of Luke is perhaps the most priceless chapter in the Bible. Certainly no chapter is more tender and more lovely. For centuries it has been called "the Gospel in the Gospels," and the story of the prodigal boy who lost everything has been known as "the pearl of the parables."

This marvelous chapter had for its original audience the indignant scribes and Pharisees. They were not interested in the Kingdom themselves, yet they were angered when they saw Jesus welcome the moral outcasts and black sheep of Jewish society. Their antagonism issued in bitter criticism and they sneered: "This fellow receives sinners and eats with them." And what does Jesus say in his defense? He does not respond with a hot protest. Rather he concedes the absolute truth of the charge, and on the basis of it presents a touching lesson in parables. The parables are three in number, with one parable including in its story another parable. Although three parables, they present one picture and they read as one continued essay on the subject of God's compassion for the lost.

The Sheep and the Coin

The first picture that Jesus sketches is that of a shepherd and his sheep. The Palestinian sheep was then and is today the so-called "broad-tailed sheep." The tails of these sheep are extremely large and weigh on an average from ten to fifteen pounds each. These sheep have always been valuable to their owners. To many of the Jews in ancient times, sheep represented their chief wealth and their sole means of livelihood. Sheep provided food to eat (1 Samuel 14:32), milk to drink (Isaiah 7:21-22), wool for the making of cloth (Job 31:20), and flesh for the offering of numerous sacrifices (Exodus 12:5,6; 20:24;

Leviticus 1:10). Because the sheep were by nature wayward and defenseless, it was necessary that they have constant supervision. In both Old and New Testaments the close relationship of God and his people is projected in the winsome figure of the shepherd and his sheep (Psalms 100:3; 23:1; Isaiah 40:11; Matthew 9:36). Thus as we read of the selfless shepherd who went out searching through the hills for one stray lamb, we should remember that Jesus Christ himself is the supremely Good Shepherd who was willing to die for his sheep (John 10:1-18).

The second picture is that of a woman who lost a coin. The coin specified by Luke was a Greek *drachma*, which was almost the equivalent of a Roman *denarius*. It was a silver coin, and although worth by our standards less than twenty cents, it was the common wage for a day's labor. Some scholars have suggested that in this case the coin was especially valuable to the woman since it formed an ornament for her head. It was customary for Jewish women to save up ten coins and string them together for a necklace or hairdress. The ornament became a treasured possession worn as the sign of a married woman, very much like a wedding band is worn today. At any rate, whether as a part of her cherished jewelry or simply as something of monetary worth, the coin was of priceless value to the woman. That is evident from her diligent search. On missing the coin, she at once lit her little oil lamp and began to sweep. A lamp was necessary for the search even in daytime, for houses then were usually built without windows and with only one door. In the house there was no wood or stone flooring, only the packed earth covered with dried reeds and rushes. With a floor like this there were many places where a coin could be lodged. All of this made the search a difficult and trying experience and helps explain why the woman was overjoyed when she found the silver piece that had been lost.

The Lost Son

The third picture that Jesus gives is that of a son. Under Jewish law the terms by which a man assigned his inheritance were quite specific. The law clearly stated that the first-born son was to receive a "double portion" of the father's property (Deuteronomy 21:17). This would mean in this case that two-thirds of the property belonged to the older son and one-third to the younger son. Often a father disposed of his possessions before he died. At the same time he conferred blessings on his sons, and these blessings were regarded as irrevocable. In the parable the younger son went to his father and demanded the part of the inheritance that was his. He wanted it right then. He could not wait. Later, after running through his fortune in the far country, he was forced to go into the field and feed swine. Since the swine were unclean animals (Leviticus 11:7), to a Jew this was the most degrading and humiliating task possible. The husks that the young man desired to eat were the pods of the carob tree, a tree that is still common in Palestine and neighboring countries. When the young man decided to return home, he intended to ask his father to treat him as a hired servant. The word used here is *misthios,* which means a hired man, a day laborer. A hired man worked only a day at a time. He had no guarantee of employment and lived on the thin edge of starvation. So a deliberate contrast in this parable is that the young man left home as a prince and returned home to be a lowly, day laborer.

Lost Men

It is good for us to try to explore these parables more fully. What do they mean? What lessons did Jesus intend to teach? In these parables Jesus taught that men are lost. It is interesting to note that Jesus seldom called men "sinners." Rather he spoke of them as being "lost" (Matthew 10:6; 15:24; 18:11). It was not that he counted them as moral wretches or outlaws in headstrong rebellion against their Maker. It was simply that men were misguided and disillusioned and needed to be set back on the right course.

There are different ways by which men become lost:

1. Sometimes a man gets lost like a sheep is lost. A sheep is a senseless and careless animal. It wanders here and there. It is apt to go any place where there is an opening. It strays off into the distant hills and does not know the way back home. It does not know that it is lost. Multitudes of people are like this. They do not revolt against God, they do not fight against his church. They edge away from him step by step. They put aside their Bibles, close their prayer-closets, and stop attending the church services. They slip away with the tide of the world and become spiritually numb. Thus the writer of the Hebrews letter warns:

"Therefore we must pay the closer attention to what we have heard, lest we drift away from it" (Hebrews 2:1). Like the heedless sheep, many men drift away from Christ.

2. Sometimes a man is lost like the coin was lost. The coin did not get lost through its own fault, but because of the fault of someone else. The woman carelessly let the coin slip through her fingers. There is a difference, of course, between coins and people. The coin was in no sense responsible for being lost. But with men there is always the responsibility of choice that governs destiny. So the coin was lost in a sense that man can never be. However, it is true that many lives end in shipwreck not primarily because of their own mistakes but because of the mistakes of others.

3. Sometimes a man is lost like the younger son was lost. The son was lost not through his own carelessness or through the carelessness of others. He took his journey to the far country with set purpose and aforethought. He turned away from home thinking of no one but himself. He never once considered the feelings of his father. Although he did not leave to hurt his father intentionally, still he was willing to break his heart in order to get his own way. Self-will is the root of sin, and it is the downfall of many souls. Deliberately, with their eyes open, many people forsake the church and go off into the land of God-forgetfulness. They throw away all restraint and violate whatever law they choose; they will eat and drink and be merry, regardless. This is the essence of sin. To desire to please self in spite of the consequences, to do what one wants to do regardless of the feelings of others, to pursue the will of self instead of the will of God, this is the heart of sin and the sin of sins. Of all the characters of literature, the younger son stands at the head of the list of those who make self-pleasing their rule of life.

God's Attitude Toward the Lost

But the main emphasis of these parables is not simply that men are lost. An even more important lesson is brought to light: God's attitude toward lost men. God's attitude toward those in sin is the same attitude that Jesus had. Jesus received sinners, and this was the very thing that the Jews could not understand. They believed that God was merciful to the righteous, but they were quite sure that he had nothing to do with sinners. The great lesson of these parables, however, is that God desires more than anything else that sinners come to him. This is shown by:

1. *The search.* God's attitude toward the lost is seen in the diligent search of the shepherd and of the woman. It is one thing to accept sinners, it is another thing to go out and look for them. A woman drops a coin. She lights a lamp and sweeps the house; she will not rest until she finds it. God is like that in his search for men. A shepherd loses one sheep from his flock. What is to be done? He leaves the ninety-nine sheep that are safe and goes out looking for it. God is like that shepherd. He wants men; and when one is lost, he goes out and finds it. He does not drive it back or hire someone to carry it back, but like the shepherd puts it on his own shoulders and brings it home. However mean and base men may be, God still wants them.

2. *The joy.* God's attitude toward the lost is seen in his joy. It is a basic point in these parables that the shepherd, the woman, and the father were filled with uncontrollable joy when they gained again what had been lost. The Pharisees had a saying, "There is joy before God when those who provoke Him perish from the world."[1] But Jesus said that there is joy in heaven before the angels of God when one sinner repents. God is kind. He is more understanding than men. He does not dismiss the tax-collectors as worthless. He feels deep in his heart the joy of joys when one wanderer returns home.

Lost But Saved

In the parable of the prodigal, Jesus tells us about a young man who threw away his life and yet was reclaimed. The downward path of the boy begins when he goes to his father to get his inheritance. He feels that he has been baby of the family long enough, and that it is time for him to strike out on his own. The father does not try to dissuade him. Anxieties that were couched in his heart, he left unexpressed. He simply let him go. And the young man left with scarcely any delay. He was off to

---

[1]Alfred Plummer, *A Critical and Exegetical Commentary on the Gospel According to St. Luke* (International Critical Commentary series; New York: Charles Scribner's Sons, n.d.) p. 371.

see the world, he would be his own master, he would please himself even if it was an affront to a gracious father.

1. *What he lost.* But the consequences of self-pleasing are always bitter. The son found out by disastrous experience what countless millions have had to learn: sin carries in itself its own penalties.

What did this young man lose when he journeyed into a far country? First, he lost the fellowship of his father and the comforts of home. He had lived in the best house, with the best servants to wait on him, under the guidance of the best father a boy could have. But all of these things meant nothing to him until he was left friendless in a strange land. A thousand miles away he dreamed of home, of his comrades in youth, and of his good father. In a far country these things were dear to him but out of his reach.

Second, he lost his self-respect. What a paradox that the young man who left home full of confidence and self-esteem was forced to go to the fields and feed swine. The boy who flung away his family because of pride ends up sleeping with swine. How different he looks now in the swine-field from that bright, clear morning when he rode away from home like a prince at the head of a caravan! His pride is shattered in the dust of the swine paths. He is unknown and unheeded and unwanted in the far country.

Third, he lost all that he had. The story says that he spent everything. The inheritance that he had received so easily he squandered easily. When he had run through his fortune and gone bankrupt, calamity struck. "A great famine arose in that country, and he began to be in want." There is, of course, always a famine in the land where God is forgotten. He finds himself alone, for his friends have deserted him. He sees now that they were not real friends. Nor were his pleasures true pleasures. They did not last.

> Pleasures are like poppies spread;
> You seize the flower, its bloom is shed.
> Or like the snow falls in the river,
> A moment white — then melts forever.[2]

---

[2]Robert Burns, *Tam o' Shanter.*

What will the prodigal do? Will he go home? No, not he; he will bear it out to the end. He takes employment from a foreign citizen. The citizen sends him to the field; now he has lost even his freedom. In fact, he has lost his independence, his pride, his fortune — everything he counted dear and for which he left home to obtain. Alone with the swine he sobs out his confession, "I perish with hunger!"

2. *How he was saved.* But this young man comes back. What were the steps on his upward journey that led him to his father? First, self-evaluation. "He came to himself." He said, "What a fool I've been. Back at home there is plenty of food. Even the servants have more to eat than I do." He was out of his mind when he left his father. He sees himself now for the first time. It is a great hour when a man comes to himself, when a man is willing to face the honest facts about himself. This is the beginning point of a man's return to God.

Second, decision. Having faced himself, the young man came to a decision. He said, "I will arise and go to my father." It was a great moment. It was a decision that for days he had pushed out of his mind. But now that he saw himself clearly, he saw his father in a different light. When we see ourselves as we are, our personal inventory should lead us to a decision of character.

Third, action. "He said I will arise....And he arose." He did not delay. He did not hesitate between saying and doing. He would not be turned aside or tempted to reconsider. He made up his mind to go, and he went. Many today are not in the body of Christ because they have floundered between the saying and the doing.

Fourth, confession. When the young man reached a decision, he worked out his confession. There would be no mincing of words or jabbering of excuses. He would speak the full truth. "Father, I have sinned against heaven and before you; I am no longer worthy to be called your son; treat me as one of your hired servants." Overwhelmed by his unworthiness, he only wants to be treated like a lowly day-laborer. He regards his sins, grievous as they were, as committed mainly against heaven and against his father. We, too, when we sin, should say like David, "Against thee, thee only, have I sinned" (Psalms 51:4).

But the confession of the humble, penitent son was cut short in the embrace of a loving father. What a painful journey it was to return home gaunt, barefooted, in rags and shame. As the prodigal rounds the bend in the road, his father recognizes him. He had been looking for him through all the sad years. He runs to him. Why did he not preserve his dignity and wait for his son to come to him? He could not! He ran to him and fell on his neck and kissed him. "Wait a minute, father," the son says. "I have sinned against heaven, I have sinned against you...." But love is so eager to receive that it does not seek explanations. The father beckons to the servants: "Bring quickly the best robe, and put it on him; and put a ring on his hand, and shoes on his feet; and bring the fatted calf and kill it, and let us eat and make merry; for this my son was dead, and is alive again; he was lost, and is found."

Saved But Lost

There is another picture in the story. The other son is out in the field. What kind of person was he? It may be that at times we deal too harshly with him.

1. He was self-righteous. He could find nothing good in the life of his brother. Everything his brother had done was bad. As for himself, he was proud of his work and proud of his life. He had worked all these years and he had not transgressed a single commandment. He was very much like the Pharisees who criticized Jesus because he received sinners.

2. He was jealous. He would not go in and greet his brother, but sulked outside the house. His father went out to him and entreated him. And what does he say? "You never gave me a kid, but look what you gave him." Of course, he had missed the mark by a mile. Not just a kid, but all that the father had was his.

3. He was heartless. He was not at all happy that his brother had come home. He would rather have his brother beaten than be forgiven. His whole outlook is one of disdain and contempt. He could not see that if his father had gained a son, he had gained a brother.

We do not deal more harshly with the older brother than the story itself. Surely no character of the Bible is more unlovely than he. The lesson of the parable is severe. It is not necessary for one to go on a long journey in order to leave God. One can stay at home — not know his Father and not know his Father's heart — and be lost at home as well as anywhere else. As Augustine prayed long ago: "It is not by our feet, or change of place, that men leave Thee ... in lustful — that is, in darkened — affections, is the true distance from Thy face."[3]

God Misses Each One

The three parables unite in teaching that God misses even one that is lost. This is true because God is a Father, and a father cannot rest until all his children are safe and secure. A father of twenty children is sad if one is missing. So God as a Father cannot spare even one. He misses each one. He yearns for his return.

> Helpless and foul as the trampled snow,
> Sinner, despair not! Christ stoopeth low
> To rescue the soul that is lost in sin,
> And raise it to life and enjoyment again.[4]

There is much hope if one's repentance, like the prodigal's, is as genuine as his fall. What a delightful sight when a prodigal returns to his Father's heart and home!

Discussion

1. What is the occasion of these parables? How is the occasion an insight into their interpretations?

2. Tell what you know of the following terms that are significant in the parables: (1) sheep, (2) *drachma*, (3) elder son, younger son, (4) husks, (5) *misthios*.

3. The parables teach something on how men become lost. What are some of the ways as indicated in the parables?

4. What points in the parables show God's attitude toward the lost?

5. What did the young man lose by leaving home? What were the steps that brought him back to his father?

6. Discuss lessons that we gain from the elder brother.

---

[3]Augustine, *Confessions* I. 28.
[4]*Beautiful Snow.* Author Unknown.

THE PARABLE OF THE DISHONEST STEWARD

"He also said to the disciples, 'There was a rich man who had a steward, and charges were brought to him that this man was wasting his goods. And he called him and said to him, "What is this that I hear about you? Turn in the account of your stewardship, for you can no longer be steward." And the steward said to himself, "What shall I do, since my master is taking the stewardship away from me? I am not strong enough to dig, and I am ashamed to beg. I have decided what to do, so that people may receive me into their houses when I am put out of the stewardship." So, summoning his master's debtors one by one, he said to the first, "How much do you owe my master?" He said, "A hundred measures of oil." And he said to him, "Take your bill, and sit down quickly and write fifty." Then he said to another, "And how much do you owe?" He said, "A hundred measures of wheat." He said to him, "Take your bill, and write eighty." The master commended the dishonest steward for his prudence; for the sons of this world are wiser in their own generation than the sons of light. And I tell you, make friends for yourselves by means of unrighteous mammon, so that when it fails they may receive you into the eternal habitations.'

" 'He who is faithful in a very little is faithful also in much; and he who is dishonest in a very little is dishonest also in much. If then you have not been faithful in the unrighteous mammon, who will entrust to you the true riches? And if you have not been faithful in that which is another's, who will give you that which is your own? No servant can serve two masters; for either he will hate the one and love the other, or he will be devoted to the one and despise the other. You cannot serve God and mammon.' "

(Luke 16:1-13)

34

Lesson 5

CHRISTIAN PRUDENCE

"The master commended the dishonest steward for his prudence." These are strange and difficult words, for they are spoken of a man who was a fraud, a trickster and a thief. Why was he commended? What lessons are to be gained by studying his schemes and watching his quick moves? Surely we need to examine this parable of Jesus very carefully.

The main character in the story is a steward who had been put in charge of a rich man's estate. The steward was probably a slave who by past service had proved himself trustworthy. As manager of the affairs, he had complete and absolute authority over everything. In time rumors reached the master's ears, and he found that his trusted slave all along had been stealing from him. At once he summoned the steward. It was a critical time. What was the steward to do? He could not establish his innocence. He had grown very careless, never anticipating that such a day would come. Was he to do manual labor? No; his hands were too soft for that. Could he find other work? There was little chance of that, for who would hire someone who had stolen from his master? Was he to beg? No; he had too much pride. He was ashamed to beg, but he was not ashamed to steal. In a flash he saw that the only way out was to steal again! He called in his master's debtors. One man owed a hundred measures of oil.[1] The steward told him to take his bill and write that he owed only fifty measures. Another man owed a hundred measures of wheat; he was told to change it to eighty.[2] In this way the steward altered the accounts of all of his master's debtors. His plan

---

[1]The measure mentioned was a *bath,* an amount equal to about five and a half American gallons.
[2]The measure here was a *cor,* equal to about five bushels.

was a simple one: by falsifying the records he figured to gain the gratitude of the debtors, so that when he was let out of his job he would be repaid by the hospitality of his friends. When his master learned of the plot, instead of burning with anger, he shrugged his shoulders and with a cynical grin commended the steward for his sharp practice. So all the characters in the story were rogues and rascals. The steward was dishonest; he had been systematically stealing from his master, and even after being caught continued to lie and steal his way out. The debtors were, of course, dishonest; they immediately seized the opportunity to take advantage of their creditor and registered their names on fictitious entries. The master also was a worldly rascal, a man who was able to appreciate a shifty bit of work even -when directed against himself.

Points of Interpretation

The parable presents indeed a peculiar story, one that has been long regarded as difficult to explain. From the outset a few points should be made clear, which aid in the interpretation of the parable.

1. The parable, although told in story form, is simply illustrative. It is not different in kind from the story of the Good Samaritan or the parable about the Prodigal Son. In each of these many details are given, but the details are added only to give force to the illustration. We are not to ask who the robbers or the innkeeper or the Samaritan represent. Likewise, in this parable we should not attach special meaning to each person and each detail. Failing to recognize this, interpreters of the past have tried, for example, to make the steward stand for such as Pilate, Judas, Satan, the Apostle Paul, and Christ himself. But the steward, the rich man, and the debtors stand for no one in particular. The parable seeks to convey one central truth, and all details of the parable must be understood in light of that truth.

2. The phrase "mammon of unrighteousness" has been made unnecessarily difficult. The word "mammon" is an Aramaic word which means "money" or "wealth." "Mammon of unrighteousness" is a descriptive phrase that means, as the Revised Standard Version has put it, "unrighteous mammon." "Unrighteous mammon" has been taken by some to mean wealth

gained by dishonest means, such as by violence or fraud. But surely Jesus does not mean that we are to make friends by means of unjust gain. Others have said that "unrighteous mammon" refers not so much to money gained illegally but to money that somehow in itself is tainted with evil, that there is a certain defilement necessarily attached to money. But the probable explanation of the problem is found in verse 12, where "unrighteous mammon" is contrasted with the "true riches." True riches are those values that are permanent and enduring: thus unrighteous mammon simply would be the untrue, the uncertain riches, the riches that cannot be trusted.

3. The commendation of the dishonest steward, it should be emphasized, came from his master. Many people get the wrong idea when they read: "And the lord commended the unjust steward, because he had done wisely" (vs. 8, King James Version). Here "the lord" does not mean "the Lord Jesus Christ," but it refers to the lord of the steward, the steward's master. Had the steward acted wisely? Not really, and so the Revised Standard Version reads: "The master commended the dishonest steward for his prudence."

Christian Prudence

Cunning and deceitful though he was, the steward is held up by Jesus as an example of Christian prudence. He said, "The sons of this world are wiser (more prudent) in their own generation than the sons of light." By this he meant that children of the world, those whose hopes are centered in material goods, have more energy and foresight in the exercise of their material concerns than Christians have in the practice of Christianity. The point is, as summarized in the words of Trench, that Christians "bestow less pains to win heaven than 'the children of this world' bestow to win earth, — that they are less provident in heavenly things than those are in earthly, — that the world is better served by its servants than God is by his."[3] Certainly that is the chief lesson of the parable. The steward bent every effort to provide for his future welfare; the debtors hastened to join in with the scheme of a crafty thief; and the master was ready to wink at their dishonesty. If Christians were as diligent

---

[3]Trench, *Notes on the Parables of Our Lord,* p. 444.

and resourceful in kingdom business as business men are in worldly business, what a marvelously different world it would be.

This chief lesson of the parable can be illustrated in various ways. Here is a man who is a golfer. He travels the circuit week after week to make a mark for himself. Before each tournament he surveys the course with scrupulous care. He practices and perfects every shot. He knows how to "fade" and "hook"; he knows when to play it safe and when to go for the pin. No matter how skilled he may be, he never plays a round without practice and often after eighteen holes he returns to the practice tee for more work on his game. Or take as another example the life insurance salesman. He studies the basic principles of salesmanship. He goes about looking for prospects; and when he finds a likely candidate, he stays with him. He calls on him time and again. He has learned that persistence pays off. If only Christians were as devoted to heavenly things as the golfer is to sharpening his strokes; if only Christians were as persistent in the pursuit of souls as the salesman is in the pursuit of money — the contrast is striking and shameful. So in this parable Jesus is saying, "Look at the way worldly men pursue their ambitions. If they are so eager about uncertain riches, why aren't you more enthusiastic about the true values?" The children of the world are more prudent than the children of light.

Management of Money

While the basic aim of the parable is to teach on Christian prudence, Jesus also uses it to teach other truths. He says, "Make friends for yourselves by means of unrighteous mammon, so that when it fails they may receive you into the eternal habitations." The expression "they may receive you" should not be pressed too far. It is merely another way of saying that if men use money in the right way, they will be received at last in heaven.

Jesus had much to say about money. In his characteristically practical way he had to give attention to man's enduring problem of the handling of money. Jesus knew that almost everything in life is measured by money. He felt it necessary, therefore, that men have a right attitude toward it. In this parable, then, what does Jesus teach concerning material wealth?

First, he says that material wealth is temporary. Unrighteous mammon is contrasted with the true riches: the true riches endure, material things do not last. Second, Jesus reminds us that our material wealth is not our own. "If you have not been faithful in that which is another's...." Even while we have it, it belongs to someone else. We have no real title to it. Its tenure is precarious; we cannot count on it for a single day. We did not bring it into the world, nor will we take it with us when we leave. It is not a part of us; we are not a part of it. It may go any day; it will go one day.

Third, Jesus teaches us that material wealth must be used wisely. Money is not a part of man. It is an adjunct, a tool that must be used in the right way. There are two very basic attitudes toward money. One attitude is that man can allow money to be his master. Man can become the slave of money. This is what happens in the case of the miser. The miser hoards all that he can get his hands on. Very recently it happened that a man called on another in the interest of raising money for a school. The man, well advanced in years, was quite wealthy, and was a citizen of the town where the school was located. One day after repeated visits had been made, the result being that not one penny had been promised to the school, the man confided in his friend. He knew, he said, that one day he was going to have to part with his money; but his money gave him so much pleasure that he could not bear the thought of it. Each evening after he closed his store, he said, he went up to his hotel room, took out his money, and ran it through his fingers. That was the only happiness that he knew. But the miser is not the only one who becomes enslaved to money. Let us remember that this happens to the man, any man, who sets the making of money above all things in life. It is well to keep in mind, as someone has pointed out, that "money can cost too much."

The other attitude toward money is that man can use it in the service of God. The grand truth underlying the whole parable is that Christians are stewards of another's possessions. That is to say, we are managers of the things that belong to God. In a very literal sense everything that we have and are — our education, our thoughts and deeds, our wealth, everything — is God's. Then it is most reasonable to use whatever is in our hands in his service. In fact, we will be found to be dishonest stewards if we selfishly treasure what is not ours. If we use our money wisely, it is to say that the supreme values in life are always human and spiritual. We never use our money in the right way until we use it in the service of God.

Fidelity in Service

Jesus attaches other lessons to this parable. He says, "He who is faithful in a very little is faithful also in much." If Christians are stewards, then it is expected of them that they be faithful (see 1 Corinthians 4:2). What does this fidelity demand? It requires that Christians be faithful in small things as well as large. If they cannot prove themselves, Jesus says, in the small things, who will commit to them the true riches? True fidelity means that Christians must continue in choosing God instead of mammon. In Biblical times no slave could serve two masters. A slave was owned absolutely by his lord; every minute of his time and every ounce of his energy belonged to him. So the Christian cannot serve God in a part-time capacity. God and mammon are uncompromising opposites. Mammon may demand, for instance, a treasuring up, while God may desire a scattering abroad. Mammon says a man is a success according to what he gets; God says a man is blessed if he gives. One must be despised if the other is to be loved. To be faithful to one means utter separation from the other. Faithful stewards are the kind of stewards that both God and man need.

Final Audit

Thus from a set of worldly rascals Jesus teaches great lessons. The men in the parable believed in things; they sought for and were absorbed in things. Nothing else mattered. The Christian, to the contrary, believes in the spiritual. He seeks the Kingdom first. Yet in all of his seeking he will miss the Kingdom, according to Jesus, if he does not pursue it with the industry and forethought of the dishonest steward. As the steward was summoned in, so the Christian will be summoned to render account of his stewardship. One last audit awaits every Christian.

Discussion

1. Tell again the story of this parable. What is unusual about the story? What are some points that make it difficult to interpret?

2. What is the central lesson of this parable? Discuss and illustrate the truthfulness of this lesson.

3. What does Jesus mean by "mammon of unrighteousness"? In what sense are we to make friends by means of it?

4. What are the two basic attitudes toward money? Are there other attitudes besides these?

5. The parable is a lesson on faithful stewardship. What is a steward? How does this parable about rascals teach on faithful stewardship?

6. What attitude toward Christian living is presented in this parable?

THE PARABLE OF THE RICH MAN AND LAZARUS

" 'There was a rich man, who was clothed in purple and fine linen and who feasted sumptously every day. And at his gate lay a poor man named Lazarus, full of sores, who desired to be fed with what fell from the rich man's table; moreover the dogs came and licked his sores. The poor man died and was carried by the angels to Abraham's bosom. The rich man also died and was buried; and in Hades, being in torment, he lifted up his eyes, and saw Abraham far off and Lazarus in his bosom. And he called out, "Father Abraham, have mercy upon me, and send Lazarus to dip the end of his finger in water and cool my tongue; for I am in anguish in this flame." But Abraham said, "Son, remember that you in your lifetime received your good things, and Lazarus in like manner evil things; but now he is comforted here, and you are in anguish. And besides all this, between us and you a great chasm has been fixed, in order that those who would pass from here to you may not be able, and none may cross from there to us." And he said, "Then I beg you, father, to send him to my father's house, for I have five brothers, so that he may warn them, lest they also come into this place of torment." But Abraham said, "They have Moses and the prophets; let them hear them." And he said, "No, father Abraham; but if some one goes to them from the dead, they will repent." He said to them, "If they do not hear Moses and the prophets, neither will they be convinced if some one should rise from the dead." ' "

(Luke 16:19-31)

Lesson 6

A GLIMPSE INTO ETERNITY

Albert Schweitzer in one of his books relates that this story started a revolution in his heart. He came to regard Africa as a beggar lying at Europe's doorstep, and so he felt that it was his mission to go to the Dark Continent. The story in Luke 16 is indeed a story that moves men to action. One can hardly read it without wondering if perhaps there might be at his own gates a neglected soul that he has never seen.

The question has often been raised whether this is a parable or an actual historical account. Some believe that it should not be understood as a parable. They point out that there is nothing in Luke's record to indicate that it is a parable, that, to the contrary, Jesus said, "There was a rich man." But the same can be said of the previous parable on the dishonest steward. Jesus began that story with exactly the same words, "There was a rich man" (Luke 16:1). It is not likely that the words should be taken figuratively in one part of the chapter and literally in another. In addition, the story of the rich man and Lazarus stands in a series of parables that reaches from Luke 14 through chapter 18. The two parables in chapter 16 are perfectly complementary to each other. They both concern the right use of money: the one showing how a wise use of wealth can secure a happy reception in heaven, the other showing how a selfish use of wealth can lead to anguish and misery in eternity.

The parable at hand is unique in at least one respect: it gives a name to one of its characters. The rich man is often known as *Dives,* which is the Latin word for rich; but this name is not a part of the parable. Jesus, however, does describe a neglected beggar and names him *Lazarus.* Lazarus was a common name, being the Greek form for the Hebrew name *Eleazar.* Eleazar means "God is my help," and no doubt Jesus selected this name to show that God is the helper of those who call on him.

Three Scenes

Jesus relates the story of the rich man and Lazarus in three scenes. There is, first, a brief picture of the two men as they lived on earth. The rich man lived in ease and luxury. He was clothed in purple and fine linen. In the ancient world purple garments were the garments of royalty and were considered a sign of honor and wealth (see Judges 8:26; Esther 8:15; Daniel 5:7). Each day the man feasted magnificently. This is what the King James Version means when it says that he "fared sumptuously." Every day he ate in royal style and arrayed himself in royal robes.

It was a very beautiful scene, except for one eyesore. At the edge of the picture, outside the gates of the palace, was a lowly beggar. He was hungry, he would gladly eat anything that came from the rich man's table. He was sick. His body was covered with loathsome ulcers. He was so weak and helpless that he could not defend himself against the dogs that licked his sores. The contrast of these two men on earth, the rich man and the beggar, is sharp and painfully tragic.

The second scene is of the two men in death. Weak and sick and hungry, it was not long till the beggar died. Was he missed? Were there friends to comfort him in the last hours? Was he extended the courtesy of a burial?

> Rattle his bones over the stones,
> He's but a pauper whom nobody owns.

The rich man also died. Everybody expected the beggar to die, but not the rich man, not the leading citizen in the town. But, like the beggar, he died. All the money that he had could not bribe away death. He died in spite of his wealth; he died in spite of his palace and fine clothes. And he was buried. What a funeral it must have been, with the gathering of crowds, the lament of mourners, and the reading of eulogies. Thus the curtain falls on the second scene of the story.

The third scene reveals the fate of the two men after death. Lazarus died and was "carried by the angels to Abraham's

44

bosom." The expression is figurative and suggests the deep fellowship of Abraham with all his true descendants: he receives them like a father encloses a child in his arms. Lazarus, therefore, was in a state of complete bliss.

The rich man, wondering where he was, lifted up his eyes in Hades. Now stripped of his purple robe, in torment, he was experiencing a foretaste of Hell. When convinced that this was really himself and not a dream, he began to plead for mercy. The rich man had become a beggar. He had sought to save his life and had lost it.

What Death Does Not Do

The parable as told by Jesus conveys great lessons concerning the life that now is and the life that is to come. It would be utterly wrong to attempt to construct, on the basis of this one parable, a detailed, inflexible theology of the after-life. The great temptation to dogmatize concerning the unknown should be avoided. Nevertheless Jesus has given us a brief look into the other world, from which there emerge certain unmistakable lessons. We learn from him that there are certain things that death, with all of its power, cannot do.

1. *Death cannot destroy consciousness.* The rich man and Lazarus are dead, and yet they are vividly alive. They are not asleep or unaware of what is about them. They are conscious.

The fact of consciousness after death is made very clear in the parable, but it is also clear from other portions of Scripture. On one occasion Jesus silenced the Sadducees, who did not believe in the resurrection, by referring to the Old Testament (see Matthew 22:23-33). He reminded them that God said to Moses, "I am the God of Abraham, and the God of Isaac, and the God of Jacob." This was long after the great patriarchs had died. Yet, Jesus adds, "God is not the God of the dead, but of the living." It is absurd to think that God rules over those who have no existence; therefore, Abraham, Isaac, and Jacob must still be living. In other places Jesus taught that consciousness survives death. He said, for example, of the wicked who rejected him and disregarded his will: "They will go away into eternal punishment" (Matthew 25:46). The place of condemnation is a place of pain and suffering. But where there is no consciousness, there is no suffering; so men are conscious after death.

2. *Death cannot destroy identity*. The rich man and Lazarus were not only alive, but they were conscious of being themselves. The rich man was still the rich man and Lazarus was still Lazarus. The rich man speaks of himself as being the same person; he knows that he is the same individual that knew Lazarus in life; and he knows that he is of a family of six brothers.

Now it is true that death changes many things. At death we are severed from all things material. Our monetary gains, our treasures, all of our possessions are wrenched from our hands. Our earthly houses are dissolved. Our bodies return to indistinguishable forms of dust. Everything that is physical perishes. But death cannot change personality. The individual self lives on.

It is remarkable how many people think that death will work for them a marvelous transformation. They feel that they can stain their lives in the slush pits of sin, and by the mere act of dying go into the presence of God as white as snow. But it is not possible to lie down one moment selfish, sinful, godless, and in the next moment after death be altogether pure and sinless and Christlike. Death's last breath cannot alter a bad character or a guilty conscience. Only the blood of Christ can cleanse a man's heart and purge his life. Death will not do for a sin-swamped soul what Christ's blood could not do. As death finds a man, so he will be the instant after when he opens his eyes in the unseen world. You will be yourself, and I will be myself. We are ourselves and will be ourselves eternally.

3. *Death cannot destroy memory*. In Hades the rich man sought relief from his anguish. But Abraham said, "Son, remember...." Abraham wanted him to look back and see the kind of person he was on earth. He could remember. He remembered his life of self-pleasing. He remembered Lazarus. He remembered his five brothers. After death, then, men will have the power of memory. The power of memory will deepen and magnify the joys of heaven; and it will also agonize the conscience and intensify the regrets of those condemned in a devil's hell.

4. *Death cannot destroy destiny*. In this story Jesus plainly teaches us that after death there are only two rewards. Lazarus found himself in a place of joy and comfort. The rich man, however, was in bitter pain. He cries that Lazarus might be sent to

touch his finger in water and cool his tongue. Even the smallest assistance would be welcomed. In the unseen realm there is a sharp separation between the God-like and the godless. There is a great gulf fixed. The Greek word for gulf is *chasma*, which is the same word as the English word chasm. Thus between the righteous and the wicked there is a huge chasm or abyss. And that chasm is fixed. The Greek word for fixed, if rendered literally, would be translated "has been and remains fixed." The division of the good and the bad is absolutely fixed and permanent.

Who separated the rich man and Lazarus? Who fixed the chasm that divided them? Not God, not Christ, not the angels. These men separated themselves. While on earth there was a great chasm that marked them off from each other. They made different choices. They traveled different roads. They lived in different worlds. And that chasm that existed on earth, unchanged by death, continued on into eternity.

The Rich Man's Condemnation

In the parable the rich man was irrevocably consigned to the place of torment. What wrongs were in his life? Why was he condemned? He was not condemned simply because he was rich or because he lived in a fine house. Not all rich people are censured by the Lord, for Abraham himself was rich. Nor was the rich man condemned because of any outright wickedness. He was not a violent man. He was not deliberately cruel to Lazarus. He did not drive him away from his gates, or slap him in the face as he passed him by. What, then, were the sins of the rich man?

1. He was indifferent. How long did Lazarus remain at the rich man's gate? We do not know, but long enough for the rich man in the afterlife to recognize Lazarus in Abraham's bosom. Time and time again the rich man had seen Lazarus begging outside his house. There right in front of him was a man sick and starving to death. That man was his responsibility. He could have emptied his pockets one day and laid up treasures in heaven. His wealth could have been the means of securing his salvation. But he was calloused to human distress, even with a man at his front door.

47

2. He was selfish. The problem of the rich man went deeper than indifference. Lying behind his cold unconcern was a self-centered life occupied with pleasures. His physical enjoyments were his chief pride. Absorbed in them, he became mercilessly oblivious to the needs of others. Selfishness degraded his life and sealed his doom.

3. He minimized the written word. When the rich man found out that no relief was possible for him, he asked that someone be sent to warn his five brothers. Abraham replied: "They have Moses and the prophets; let them hear them." "No father Abraham," he said, "that is not enough." It was as though to say, "If I had been rightly warned, if something else had been offered to me besides Moses and the prophets, I would have listened." Thus on earth the rich man made light of the word of God. He had looked on it as powerless and peripheral. But Abraham said that God's written message was as effective as a voice from the dead.

Men are not saved by the witness of ghosts. They are not convinced through miracles but by persuasion. God draws men to Christ through the teaching of his word (John 6:44-45). The word of God when believed and received is able to save from sin (James 1:21). To underestimate its value is to put oneself in jeopardy of everlasting rejection.

Discussion

1. Review the pros and cons as to whether this is a parable or not. If it is a parable, what is unusual about it? What do the names *Dives* and *Lazarus* mean?

2. Discuss what is meant by the following: (1) "fared sumptuously," (2) Abraham's bosom, (3) Hades. Is this story a picture of death before or after the Judgment Day? Give reasons for your answer.

3. How does this parable teach consciousness and personal identity after death? What other Scriptures teach the same lessons?

4. Discuss the statement "There is a great gulf fixed." What lessons are to be gained here?

5. Why was the rich man condemned? In what ways does he serve as a warning to us?

6. Does one have to be very wealthy to be condemned for the rich man's sin?

48

THE PARABLE OF THE PHARISEE AND
THE PUBLICAN

"He also told this parable to some who trusted in themselves that they were righteous and despised others: 'Two men went up into the temple to pray, one a Pharisee and the other a tax collector. The Pharisee stood and prayed thus with himself, "God, I thank thee that I am not like other men, extortioners, unjust, adulterers, or even like this tax collector. I fast twice a week, I give tithes of all that I get." But the tax collector, standing far off, would not even lift up his eyes to heaven, but beat his breast, saying, "God, be merciful to me a sinner!" I tell you, this man went down to his house justified rather than the other; for every one who exalts himself will be humbled, but he who humbles himself will be exalted.' "

(Luke 18:9-14)

Lesson 7

"GOD BE MERCIFUL"

In chapter 18 of Luke there are two parables on prayer. The first one is about a widow who continued to bother a judge until finally he had to hear her case. In this parable Jesus teaches that his disciples should be as persistent in prayer as the widow was in her complaint. The second parable, which allows us to see two men at worship, is directed against all sorts of pretentious parade in religion. This parable was originally spoken for those "who trusted in themselves that they were righteous and despised others."

The Two Men

This story, like so many of Jesus' stories, brings into view a set of articulate contrasts. There is, first of all, the contrast between the two men who went to the temple to pray. One man was a Pharisee. The name Pharisee stood for one who was separate from others. The Pharisees insisted on the meticulous observance of the law, and they set themselves apart from the ordinary people whom they called "the people of the land." They were strict legalists. They regarded themselves as protectors of the law; they were accused of "building a fence around the law," which meant that they built around the law a wall of their own traditions. They analyzed the law to death. Jesus said they made void the word of God by their traditions (Matthew 15:6; Mark 7:8ff).

Numerous illustrations could be given to show how the Pharisees "fenced" the law through their traditions. Take, for example, the matter of the washing of hands. This was considered a religious rite by the Pharisees, and there were very rigid regulations that had to be followed. It was necessary that the water drawn be as pure as possible; it was not to be defiled by using part of it for some other purpose. In each washing the minimum amount of water permissible was a quarter of a log, equal to about one and a half eggshells. The water was poured over both hands. In order that the entire hand might be washed, the hands were lifted up to make the water run down to the wrist. After one hand was cleansed, it could be used to rub the other hand. Then followed a second washing, this time the hands being held down to allow the water to drop off of the finger tips. The purpose of the second washing was to rinse away the water that had touched the defiled hands in the first washing.[1]

These pedantic regulations were characteristic of the Pharisees in the first century. So when Jesus describes a Pharisee as going to the temple to worship, a vivid picture comes to our minds. The Pharisee is a supremely religious man, He comes to the temple at the precise hour of prayer. He sweeps up the steps with a lordly look, all eyes watching him. He enters the Court of Israel and draws near to the altar of burnt offering. He stands erect, displays his broad phylacteries, looks around at others, and begins to phrase certain familiar words.

The other man was a tax collector. While the Jews were under Roman domination, there were many taxes they had to pay. There was a land tax, which was payable in produce or money. There was a poll tax and a tax on personal property, which every person had to pay. There were export and import customs, tolls charged at harbors, roads, bridges, city gates, and so forth. To gather these various taxes, the Romans borrowed a method of tax-collecting used by the Ptolemies of Egypt. Instead of sending their own officials in to exact payment, they contracted with others the right to collect taxes. For a given locality a definite sum would be agreed upon, and anything collected above that would go to those who contracted the taxes. These contractors had numerous assistants working for them in the actual collecting of the taxes. The subordinates were the despised publicans or tax collectors mentioned in the New Testament.[2]

---

[1] Alfred Edersheim, *The Life and Times of Jesus the Messiah,* II, pp. 10-12.
[2] See the articles "Tax, Taxes," "Tax Collector" in *The Interpreter's Dictionary of the Bible* (New York: Abingdon Press, 1962), IV, pp. 520-22.

Tax authorities are always unpopular, and this was especially so for the tax collectors in the land of Palestine. The proud Jewish people deeply resented their being subjects of Rome. Radical factions among them maintained that to pay tribute to Caesar was to commit treason against God. Thus tax collectors were not merely the representatives of a foreign government; in the eyes of many Jews they had sold themselves out to the oppressor, and this they had done at the expense of their own countrymen. Besides, the tax collectors were notoriously dishonest. Many of the people did not know the tax laws, and often under the guise of some unread law the tax collectors would literally steal everything they had. To be a tax collector, therefore, was to be counted as the lowest and meanest of all sinners.

So the two men who went into the temple were at opposite poles. The Pharisee was on the top rung of the social ladder, the tax collector was at the bottom. One man was respected and honored, the other was an outcast, a traitor and a robber. How amazing it is, then, that Jesus dared to compare them. And how revealing the comparison is as we overhear their prayers.

The Two Prayers

The Pharisee took his customary position and, with raised chin, spoke words that laid bare his inner self. "God, I thank thee that I am not like other men, extortioners, unjust, adulterers, or even like this tax collector. I fast twice a week, I give tithes of all that I get." What kind of prayer is this? Why was it uttered in vain?

1. The Pharisee's prayer was a prayer of imperfect goodness. Much of it consisted of negative conduct. The man found pleasure with himself because of certain things he had not done. He was not guilty of extortion, nor was he dishonest or immoral. Even his fasting and tithing were in a sense negative, for these were things that he had given up. Thus the Pharisee lived by the negative of the Golden Rule. It was the accepted rule of life at that time. Rabbi Hillel, who died in the beginning of the Christian era, had done much to popularize it. Once a Gentile came to him and said that he would become a proselyte if he could teach him the whole law while standing on one leg. Rabbi Hillel, shifting his weight to one foot, answered: "Do not to thy

neighbor what is disagreeable to thee."[3] Living by this rule the Pharisee had become quite self-satisfied. His negative religion had left him content with himself, and he was perfectly sure that if anybody had gained heaven it was he. In addition, he made the mistake of measuring himself by the other fellow. He was always scrutinizing others. It is significant that as he prays his eyes rove about until he sees the tax collector. As compared with him, of course, he is a saint. It was not much to his credit that he was better than a tax collector. By the cheap method of making others look bad, he made himself look good. But he was the loser, for he was blinded to his sinful self.

2. The Pharisee's prayer was a prayer of pride and self reassurance. His first words are that he is thankful for not being like other men. What an odious way to begin a prayer! It is as much as to say, "Look at me. God, what a splendid person I am!" He speaks not out of gratitude, but as though he would invite God to join in admiration of himself. He must tell himself and God how good he is. There was nothing in his prayer but "I." He was only concerned with what "I" had done and had not done. He could list all the things under the sun that he had not engaged in. He could boast to himself that he fasted twice a week. The Pharisees usually fasted on Mondays and Thursdays, for Moses was supposed to have ascended Mt. Sinai on a Monday and descended on a Thursday. To fast twice a week was much more than the minimum requirement; according to the Jewish law, the Day of Atonement was the only day in the year that demanded a fast. The Pharisee could also boast to himself that he gave tithes of everything he acquired. Undoubtedly this included tithes of petty things, like herbs of mint and dill (see Matthew 23:23). Even the tithing of trifles contributed to his conceit. He was very proud that he had not omitted keeping the least of the commandments. Therefore, he does not in all of his prayer ask a petition of God. Does he seek the pardon of his sins? Does he ask for divine strength or guidance? No! He sees the publican over in the corner of the temple court. Does he pray for him? Absolutely not! He does not ask because he wants to believe that he is in want of nothing. He does not need God. It is little wonder, then, that Jesus introduces him by saying that "he prayed with himself." He spoke in the circle of "I." Sepa-

---

[3]Cited by Schaff, *History of the Christian Church*, I, p. 161.

rated from others and separated from God, he prayed to convince himself that he was a righteous man.

How refreshingly different is the prayer of the tax collector. He has not darkened the door of the temple in years. He does not come now for show. He is in trouble. He needs help. He must go to God. But he is not sure that he will be heard. He stands far removed from the altar, with his head dropped between his shoulders. He will not cast a glance to heaven. In sorrow and agony he beats his breast. What can he say? How shall he begin to express the feeling in his soul? Finally he cries, "God, be merciful to me a sinner!" In the Greek language the definite article is attached to sinner, not a sinner, but the sinner. He regards himself as the worst of sinners, the sinner of sinners. His prayer was not a long prayer, only seven words; but it went to the heart of the matter, and was unsurpassably sincere.

The Two Results

As the two prayers were different, so the results of the prayers were different. Jesus pronounces judgment on the men.. "I say to you," speaking with his characteristic authority, "this man (the tax collector) went down to his house justified rather than the other." One man was justified; the other was not. One prayer went up like incense before God; the other like a cold wintry wind was blown back in the face of its offerer. In the temple, in the presence of God, the Pharisee had stood, and had gone away "unhelped and unblessed." He went home with the same dead heart as he had before. The next day probably found him once again in the temple praying with himself, self-praised and self-condemned.

It was not a prayerless prayer that the tax collector expressed. He had gone up to the temple because he needed to go. Things were not right, and he wanted to make them right. He came to establish a right relationship with God, and, according to Jesus, that relationship was established. He went home relieved, forgiven, cleansed. He had prayed like the psalmist:

> Evils have encompassed me without number;
> My iniquities have overtaken me till I cannot see;
> They are more than the hairs of my head;
> My heart fails me.
>
> (Psalms 40:12)

He had prayed as Ezra had prayed: "O my God, I am ashamed and blush to lift my face to thee, my God, for our iniquities have risen higher than our heads, and our guilt has mounted up to the heavens" (Ezra 9:6). He had prayed the simple prayer that all men need to pray, "God, be merciful to me the sinner!"

Discussion

1. Who were the Pharisees? What was their attitude toward others? Describe their traditions.

2. Why were the tax collectors so despised? What method did the Romans use to collect their taxes? What were some of these taxes?

3. What was wrong with the Pharisee's prayer? The Bible says that "he prayed with himself." What does this mean?

4. Contrast the results of the two prayers. What do you think was the difference between the prayers?

5. Is this parable directed most at teaching attitudes behind prayer? Is it possible for Christians to have the Pharisee's attitude in activities other than prayer?

THE PARABLE OF THE LABORERS IN
THE VINEYARD

"Then Peter said in reply, 'Lo, we have left everything and followed you. What then shall we have?' Jesus said to them, 'Truly, I say to you, in the new world, when the Son of man shall sit on his glorious throne, you who have followed me will also sit on twelve thrones, judging the twelve tribes of Israel. And every one who has left houses or brothers or sisters or father or mother or children or lands, for my name's sake, will receive a hundredfold, and inherit eternal life. But many that are first will be last, and the last first.

" 'For the kingdom of heaven is like a householder who went out early in the morning to hire laborers for his vineyard. After agreeing with the laborers for a denarius a day, he sent them into his vineyard. And going out about the third hour he saw others standing idle in the market-place; and to them he said, "You go into the vineyard too, and whatever is right I will give you." So they went. Going out again about the sixth hour and the ninth hour, he did the same. And about the eleventh hour he went out and found others standing and he said to them. "Why do you stand here idle all day?" They said to him, "Because no one has hired us." He said to them, "You go into the vineyard, too." And when evening came, the owner of the vineyard said to his steward, "Call the laborers and pay them their wages, beginning with the last up to the first." And when those hired about the eleventh hour came, each of them received a denarius. Now when the first came, they thought they would receive more; but each of them also received a denarius. And on receiving it they grumbled at the householder, saying, "These last worked only one hour, and you have made them equal to us who have borne the burden of the day and the scorching heat." But he replied to one of them, "Friend, I am doing you no wrong; did you not agree with me for a denarius? Take what belongs to you, and go; I choose to give to this last as I give to you. Am I not allowed to do what I choose with what belongs to me? Or do you begrudge my generosity?" So the last will be first, and the first last.' "

(Matthew 19:27-20:16)

Lesson 8

UNDESERVED FAVOR

We are confronted here with the most puzzling of all the parables. The story, on the face of it, is very improbable; and were it not told by Jesus, we would hesitate to believe it. The owner of a vineyard went out early in the morning looking for workers. Finding some men available, he talked with them, and they agreed to work for a denarius each. The denarius was a Roman coin worth about twenty cents and was the ordinary pay for a day laborer. In all of this there is nothing unusual, for in Palestine a man was hired at dawn and paid at sunset. The early morning hours passed; and because there was much work to be done, the owner goes again to the market-place in search of laborers. According to the story, he finds men at the third, the sixth, the ninth, and the eleventh hours. The Jews divided the daytime into twelve equal parts. The length of the hour depended on the length of the day. The third hour would be approximately 9 a.m., the sixth hour about noon, the ninth hour mid-afternoon, and the eleventh hour about 5 p.m. It is important to notice that as the owner contacts the different laborers through the day, no bargain on pay is reached with them. The owner simply says that he will treat them right at the end of the day. It is also important to notice that the owner hires all the men he finds, and that none of the men when found refuse to go into the vineyard. They evidently did not feel that they were in a position to bargain; they only wanted a chance to work, and they were willing to commit themselves to the goodness of the owner.

It is at the close of the day that we come face to face with the eccentric lord. The law of Moses stated that a hired man was to be paid at the day's end. Speaking of the laborer, the law read: "You shall give him his hire on the day he earns it, before the sun goes down" (Deuteronomy 24:15; see also Leviticus 19:13). So the laborers were called and given their wages; and, strangely, those who had come into the vineyard last were paid first. Not only so, but the five o'clock men were paid for the full day's work. How surprised and happy they were! What had been a long, fruitless day, as they looked for work, has now been turned into joy by a generous lord. The others employed at different hours were likewise well-treated: they were paid in full, although they had only worked in part. Then the time came to pay those who had worked the entire day. Since the lord had been so gracious, paying as much as a denarius for one hour's work, they expected to get more. But they, too, received the same wages. With bitterness they object, "Have we not borne the burden of the day and the scorching sun? Why have you not been as liberal with us as with the others?" The answer flew back, "I do you no wrong. You have what we agreed upon; take your money and go."

Was the Owner Unjust?

What strikes us first about the parable is that apparently the owner of the vineyard was unjust. We are ready to argue that the men who laborered in the heat of the day ought to be paid more than the late-comers. We instinctively have a kind of pity for the grumblers. In order to justify, therefore, the unusual actions of the owner, various explanations have been proposed. It has been said, for example, that the owner's conduct can be explained on the grounds that the late workers did as much in one hour as the early workers did in twelve. But there is no hint of this in the parable. Others have sought to explain the difficulty by assuming that some workers were paid with a brass denarius, and others with a silver or gold denarius. But this interpretation contradicts the parable itself, for we may be sure that no objection would have been forthcoming had each of the early workers received a gold denarius. Thus we must look elsewhere for the correct explanation. It must be granted that all the workers were not treated on the same basis. The owner himself acknowledges this. "Am I not allowed," he asks, "to do what I choose with what belongs to me?" But if the owner's methods represented unequal treatment, they did not represent unfair treatment. He did not wrong the early workers by doing a favor to their fellows. He did not withhold from them one cent of what was theirs. The trouble with the early workers was that they were jealous over what the others had received. They simply begrudged the owner's generosity. They murmured not because the lord had deprived them, but because he had been so merciful to the others.

The Original Warnings

It should always be kept in mind that this parable was addressed directly to the apostles. In the previous chapter (Matthew 19), we read of a young man who came to Jesus in quest of eternal life. He was a good man, he had kept all the commandments of the law from his youth. Yet one thing he lacked. Jesus said that he needed to sell whatever he had, give it to the poor, and come and follow him. The young man, clinging to this many possessions, went away sorrowfully. Then Peter, unaware of his self-righteous pretension, drew a contrast of himself and the apostles with the self-centered rich man. He said, "Lo, we have left everything and followed you. What then shall we have?" Jesus responded that they, and all others who forsake themselves, will be greatly compensated — a hundredfold in this world and eternal life in the world to come. But lest Peter get the wrong impression, Jesus hastened to add, "Many that are first will be last, and the last first." That is to say, "Do not be so much concerned about what you are going to get. In the kingdom of heaven it is not a matter of punching the clock, so much work and so much reward. If that is your attitude, great as your work may be, it will be small in the sight of God. Men may regard you first, but God will regard you last." Then Jesus gave the parable as an illustration of what he meant. The first hired were the last paid and the least honored. Not simply because they were first were they made last, but because they had the wrong spirit of work. When so understood, the parable becomes a warning to the apostles who, as the first workers in the vineyard, might through an improper spirit end up as last in the kingdom.

The parable also may be taken as a warning to the Jews. The Jews had for centuries looked upon themselves as the elect people of God. They were bound to God by a special covenant, and they were the exclusive recipients of his special promises. Very early they had entered the Lord's vineyard. All other nations were latecomers. So according to this view, Jesus is saying that the Jews, like the early workers, would resent the gathering in of the Gentiles. Last in time to come into the kingdom, the Gentiles through their service would be made first; and the Jews, who were once first, because of their hatred of others would be made last. Certainly this interpretation has some merit, especially when it is remembered that the parable stands in a series of parables that have to do with the Jews' rejection of God's kingdom.

Attitude Toward Work

Aside from its primary applications to the disciples and to the Jewish nation, the parable plainly teaches other basic truths. It tells us that the amount of work accomplished is not as important as the spirit with which the work is done. In the parable we see two types of workers. There are, on one hand, the workers who work for pay. It is specifically said that the early workers agreed to work for a denarius a day. This may suggest that there was some bargaining on both sides. At least it means that they did not set to work until definite terms were met. Many people are like that. On almost every job and in practically every business or profession, there are those who work only for pay. They have decided on their vocation or taken their job with one thing uppermost in their minds: "How much am I going to get?" With this one self-absorbed aim they do their tasks. For them work is a duty, a burden that has to be borne; and other than doing what they are told to do, they yield naked nothing. A teacher who teaches for gain, a doctor who is more concerned about collecting his bills than tending his patients, a preacher who first looks at the paycheck before setting out for a new field, are sowing the seeds of decay in a society they profess to serve. Likewise, in spiritual matters, many people work for pay. They want to deal with the Lord on the principle of so much for so much. They picture God as a ledger-keeper who puts down in the credit column so many hours of work and so many deeds done. This was the attitude that Peter had. "Lord, look at the hard lives we've had to live and the sacrifices we've had to make in following you. Now, tell us what we will get." Peter had the hireling spirit, a spirit which if unchanged would cause him to be last in the kingdom.

On the other hand, there were the workers who work without thinking of the pay. The workers employed in the late hours did not require an agreement before entering the vineyard. They depended solely on the generosity of the owner. It was enough for him to say, "Whatever is right I will give you." They did their work, trusting that the master would reward them. True Christian service must always be rendered in that spirit. The man who really serves God does not serve for pay. Love seeks no reward. The mother who guards the bed of a sick child does not think of reward. Parents who plan and save and pray for their children do not expect reward. Love secures its joy in bending low to the poor, in speaking words of encouragement to the depressed, and in sharing a comfortable home with a friend. A legendary but beautiful story is related of Thomas Aquinas. While engaged in worship one day, it is said that a heavenly voice addressed him: "Thomas, thou has written much and well concerning me. What reward shall I give thee for thy work?" Thomas answered, "Nothing but thyself, O Lord." The true Christian does not worry about reward. He leaves it up to God. He knows that to be with God in eternity is the greatest of all rewards.

The Grace of God

In the parable the workers all received the same pay, no matter what hour they went into the vineyard. Those that worked only one hour received pay for a full day. They did not earn it, but still they received it. They received it because the owner was gracious and good. Surely the lesson here is unmistakably clear. We do not earn what God gives us. We do not deserve his long-suffering with us. He does not owe a single one of us his salvation. The English preacher John Newton once said: "When I get to heaven I shall see three wonders. The first will be to see many persons there whom I did not expect to see; the second will be to miss many whom I did expect to see; the greatest wonder of all will be to find myself there." We work, it is true, but what God gives is not pay. Salvation is a gift of his grace.

Discussion

1. Why is this parable regarded as difficult? What unusual features are in this parable?

2. Discuss the justice of the owner of the vineyard. What interpretations have been suggested to get around the owner's apparent injustice? Was the owner unjust to any of his workers?

3. To whom was this parable originally addressed? In its original setting, the parable served as a warning to what two groups?

4. What does this parable teach about attitudes? What does it teach about God's grace?

5. Would the justice of the vineyard owner work in today's business world?

6. Should a store owner pay the most to those who work hardest and longest? Should the Lord reward on the same basis? What is the difference?

THE PARABLE OF THE TWO SONS

" 'What do you think? A man had two sons; and he went to the first and said, "Son, go and work in the vineyard today." And he answered, "I will not"; but afterward he repented and went. And he went to the second and said the same; and he answered, "I go, sir," but did not go. Which of the two did the will of his father?' They said, 'The first.' Jesus said to them, 'Truly, I say to you, the tax collectors and the harlots go into the kingdom of God before you. For John came to you in the way of righteousness, and you did not believe him, but the tax collectors and the harlots believed him; and even when you saw it, you did not afterward repent and believe him.' "

(Matthew 21:28-32)

Lesson 9

THE TEST OF TWO SONS

This parable in an extraordinary way reveals Jesus as the Master Teacher. Gathered around him were a group of Jews who were seeking his destruction. For their benefit he told a story, and then he asked their opinion of it. The answer they gave was perfectly correct, unaware of the story's implications. Not until it was finished did they realize that their response had accused themselves and had fixed their own punishment.

The story is about a father who had a vineyard. He went to his two sons and asked them to work for him. The first son bluntly refused, but later changed his mind and went. The second son readily agreed to work but never kept his promise. "Of the two sons," Jesus asked, "which did the will of his father?" It was an incisive question that demanded an answer.

The meaning of the parable is crystal clear. The first son who would not work and later decided to work stands for the tax collectors and sinners. All their lives by their wicked deeds they had been saying no to God; yet when Jesus came they could no longer persist in sin but pressed to enter the kingdom. The second son represents the leaders of the Jews, the Pharisees and the Sadducees, who were always making the pretense of serving God, but when Jesus came they despised his teachings and finally crucified him. They had rejected John, they rejected Jesus. Tax collectors and sinners had turned from their ways, but the Jewish aristocracy had made no amends and had cast aside the heavenly kingdom.

The parable is rich in content and suggests a number of practical lessons beyond its original application. These lessons may be grouped around three ideas: the call, the work, and the workers.

The Call

One of the first things that impresses us in this parable is the direct way the father approaches this sons. He feels that he has the right to ask them to go into his vineyard. He speaks to both in the kindest of terms and says, "Son, go work!" In this way God as Father gently calls all men. It is God who is ever seeking workers; it is God who takes the initiative to bring the inactive and indifferent into his vineyard. Jesus speaks of this divine impulse. He says, pointing to himself, "No one can come to me unless the Father who sent me draws him" (John 6:44). God draws men to the Savior. How does he accomplish this? It is not through a weird dream or a fantastic vision that God reaches men. It is not by the ouija board or the crystal ball. What is his drawing power? Jesus continues and explains: "It is written in the prophets, 'And they shall all be taught by God.' Every one who has heard and learned from the Father comes to me" (vs. 45). Thus God draws men through teaching. Paul the Apostle said that men are called by means of the gospel (2 Thessalonians 2:14). Men are brought near the fountain of grace when they learn and receive and submit to the gospel of Christ.

It is significant that the father who had only two sons asked each of them to work. God's call goes out to all his children. It is as world-wide as human flesh. It is as all-pervading as human needs. It speaks to the cheerless and downtrodden and says, "Come to me, all ye that labor and are heavy laden, and I will give you rest" (Matthew 11:28). It summons disciples to evangelize the nations. Not a soul is to be left out. The call is universal, and it is individual. God speaks to you and to me. He bids us one by one. He wants all his children to enter his vineyard, and when one does not enter in, it is a flat refusal to acknowledge his authority.

The Work

What did the Father desire his sons to do? He asked them to work in the vineyard. The call from God, then, is a call for men to work. It is not a call to rest and ease. Tennyson in his poem *The Lotos-Eaters* retells the story found in the *Odyssey* of Ulysses' visit to an enchanting land that was "always afternoon." There the sailors came and ate of the unusual Lotos plant; and after tasting its sweet fruit, all they wanted to do

was to sleep and dream and live with half-shut eyes. And so
they say:

> Surely, surely, slumber is more sweet than toil, the
> shore
> Than labor in the deep mid-ocean, wind and wave
> and oar;
> O, rest ye, brother mariners, we will not wander
> more.

They had lost all desire to return to their homeland and were
perfectly content to recline on the hills with their dreams.
Many people today in Christ's vineyard are like the Lotos-
eaters, content to bask in the sunshine of indolence. They do not
realize what being a Christian demands. They have entered the
Lord's church like people run to a shelter to escape a storm; and
when once inside, they just stand around and watch it rain. It is
true, of course, that there is a certain measure of safety and
protection in the church, and that among God's people one can
find much strength for his soul; but the church, like a vineyard,
is a place of work, and all of those in the vineyard should be
engaged in its program of work. We say that we are Christians,
but often we do not spend fifteen minutes during the week
working at the job. We say that we are Christians, and yet
many times we are too lazy to visit someone who is in the death-
grip of sin. It must not be forgotten that the Lord's vineyard is a
place where work is to be done.

But the call of the father to his sons had a sense of urgency
about it. "Go and work in the vineyard today." Work needed to
be done, and it needed to be done that day. So Christ's call is for
men who will work for him today. That is, after all, the only
time there is. Yesterday is gone forever, and we dare not boast
of tomorrow (Proverbs 27:1). Today is all that we have. It is our
one chance, our one opportunity to serve. "Behold, now is the
acceptable time; behold, now is the day of salvation" (2 Corinthians 6:2). If we hold back and procrastinate, if we wait until
tomorrow to do the work of today, the chances are the work will
never be done; and in effect we are like the son who bluntly said
to this father, "I will not."

The Workers

It is interesting to see how the two sons respond to the
father's command. One son is very polite and respectful. When

asked to work he gives an immediate reply, "I go, sir." Though his brother might refuse his father, he would not. He would go. How courteous he is. And how sure he is that he will succeed.

Why, then, did he fail his father? Why at the end of the day had he not gone near the vineyard? It was not that he had deliberately deceived his father. He had worked out no plot of intrigue by which he hoped to bankrupt his father. He did not purposefully lie to him. He purposed to obey him. In his father's presence he really intended to go to the vineyard, but in his absence he found that the doing of the task was more difficult than the saying of the words.

This son represents, therefore, that large host of Christ's would-be followers who profess much and practice little. Many people, like the son, pledge their loyal service to the Master and then fall down on their pledge. From its earliest times the church has always been plagued by this problem. In the first century there was a group of pseudo-Christians who were called the Gnostics. They made great professions. They prided themselves on their fellowship with God, on their walking in the light, on their living above sin. These were glowing words. Yet many of them lived in the depths of sin; no physical appetite or immoral desire was forbidden to them. To counteract such perversity, John writes that, "God is light, and in him is no darkness at all" and that "he who says 'I know him' but disobeys his commandments is a liar, and the truth is not in him" (1 John 1:5; 2:4). The Gnostics also spoke of knowing God and of loving God, yet they had contempt in their hearts for their Christian brothers. This, John says, they could not do. They must love their brothers (1 John 4:7-21; 3:11-18), and their love must be genuine. John exhorts: "Little children, let us not love in word or speech but in deed and in truth" (1 John 3:18). Thus in the early church there were those who praised love but did not practice love.

Profession without practice, promise without performance, — these continue to be the greatest enemies of the cause of Christ. Mohandas K. Gandhi, who was born a Hindu, spent much of his life in the study of comparative religions. In Christianity he found many teachings that appealed to him, and many Christian people became his friends. Of these people he often spoke warmly. But in his *Autobiography* he tells of several disappointing visits which he made to a church in Pretoria, South Africa. There he found the people only half-heartedly interested in the Christianity they professed. Of them Gandhi wrote: "The church did not make a favourable impression on me. The sermons seemed to be uninspiring. The congregation did not strike me as being particularly religious. They were not an assembly of devout souls; they appeared rather to be worldly-minded people, going to church for recreation and in conformity to custom. Here, at times, I would involuntarily doze. I was ashamed, but some of my neighbors, who were in no better case, lightened the same. I could not go on long like this and soon gave up attending the service."[1] It is a sad passage in an immensely interesting autobiography. A man who was to become one of the world's great leaders was hindered in his search for truth by the undesirable lives of those who claimed to be Christians.

The other son refused his father and curtly said, "I will not." He offered no reason or excuse. He was not going. Many people are like this son. When the Father calls them to enter his vineyard, they bluntly refuse. They say that they will have nothing to do with any kind of church. They do not excuse their sins. In fact, they speak of their sins freely, as though a frank confession of their immorality can serve as a substitute for their obedience. But in the Last Day what comfort will there be to the lost man who openly traveled the highway to destruction? A man is no less a sinner when he admits that he is not a saint.

The son, however, made a change for the better. He remembered his ugly mood and the blatant discourtesy he had shown his father. He had begun the day badly. But having begun wrong, he saw no reason to continue in the wrong. So he repented. Of what did his repentance consist? It was more than simply a twinge of sorrow because he denied his father. He could have grieved much without repenting. When did he repent? Only when he changed his mind, when he turned in the opposite direction, and when he actually went to work in the father's vineyard!

---

[1]M. K. Gandhi, *Gandhi's Autobiography.* First written in Gujarati under the title *The Story of My Experiments with Truth*; translated by Mahadev Desai. (Washington, D. C.: Public Affairs Press, 1948), p. 198-99.

Which of the Two?

Jesus asked which of the two sons did the will of his father. There is a world of emphasis on the word *did.* Of all things that could be said about them, the only important thing, according to Jesus, is whether the sons did the will of their father. All else is of no consequence. No matter how good the intentions, no matter how many the promises, the simple fact is that one son did and one son did not. Fine words can never take the place of fine deeds.

Discussion

1. What was the original application of this parable? Whom did the two sons represent?

2. This parable teaches that God calls men into his vineyard. Discuss the nature of this call and its significance.

3. What were the sons called to do? When were they to begin? What lessons are to be gained here?

4. What types of persons today are similar to the two sons?

5. What does this parable teach on repentance?

6. What different types of work are there in God's "vineyard"? Is bearing a burden patiently "work"?

THE PARABLE OF THE WICKED HUSBANDMEN

" 'Hear another parable. There was a householder who planted a vineyard, and set a hedge around it, and dug a wine press in it, and built a tower, and let it out to tenants, and went into another country. When the season of fruit drew near, he sent his servants to the tenants, to get his fruit; and the tenants took his servants and beat one, killed another, and stoned another. Again he sent other servants, more than the first; and they did the same to them. Afterward he sent his son to them, saying, "They will respect my son." But when the tenants saw the son, they said to themselves, "This is the heir; come, let us kill him and have his inheritance." And they took him and cast him out of the vineyard, and killed him. When therefore the owner of the vineyard comes, what will he do to those tenants?' They said to him, 'He will put those wretches to a miserable death, and let out the vineyard to other tenants who will give him the fruits in their season.'

"Jesus said to them, 'Have you never read in the scriptures:
The very stone which the builders rejected
has become the head of the corner;
this was the Lord's doing,
and it is marvelous in our eyes?
Therefore I tell you, the kingdom of God will be taken away from you and given to a nation producing the fruits of it.' "

(Matthew 21:33-43)
(Parallel passages: Mark 12:1-12; Luke 20:9-18)

70

THE GOODNESS AND SEVERITY
OF GOD

When Jesus spoke this parable, his hour had come. Throughout his ministry he had spoken of his time and his hour (John 2:4; 7:6,8; 12:23). All through his life Jesus knew that he had come for a specific purpose and to accomplish a specific work. It was his unique task to bring to consumation the grand purposes of God for a lost world. In his public preaching, however, it would have been disastrous for him to have announced that he was Messiah. Messiah was a term that made all of Palestine bristle with patriotic fervor, that incited head-strong enthusiasts to such heights that they wanted to take up arms and drive the Roman legions out from their country. So it was necessary for Jesus to avoid a public use of the term. But as the time drew near for him to face death, Jesus talked more freely about his real nature. When finally his hour arrived, with deliberate calculation and according to a set plan, he went to Jerusalem to die. He entered Jerusalem in triumph and was openly proclaimed as Messiah. He went into the temple and with reckless abandon overthrew the tables of the money-changers. He refused to tell by what authority he was doing these things. He took matters into his own hands. And now that he was teaching in the temple, he forced the issue with the Parable of the Wicked Husbandmen.

The Parable

The story that Jesus told brought familiar pictures to mind in his audience. The land of Judea was a land of many vineyards. According to Jesus' story, the householder took great care in preparing his vineyard. The plot of land was made ready. Large stones were removed and the ground was plowed.

The vines were planted, and around it was placed a hedge to protect the vineyard from wild animals and thieves. The hedge was either a thorn hedge or a stone wall. A wine press was made. The ordinary press consisted of two pits which were dug out of rocky ground. The pits, which were connected by a channel, were so constructed that one pit was higher than the other. The grapes were pressed by foot in the higher vat, and the juice was allowed to drain down into the lower. A tower also was built, probably made of stone. It was used to provide lodging for the workers and also as a lookout against possible robbers during the harvest time. Having equipped the vineyard, the householder rented it out to tenants and went away into a far country. In those days Palestine was a troubled land, and it was nothing unusual for a man to leave his property in the care of others and go and live abroad. Rent from the land was derived in one of three ways. The tenant might give a stated amount of money to the owner; or he might pay a certain amount of produce, whether the harvest was good or bad; or he might agree to share in a certain portion of the fruit, usually one-third or one-fourth of the harvest.[1] But in the parable the tenants continually refused to pay their rent. Not only so, but they shamefully wronged the representatives that were sent to them, and at last they murdered the owner's beloved son. There is here also a sad touch of realism in the story, for in Palestine land-renters frequently abused the legitimate rights of absentee landlords. So the story that Jesus told was the kind of story that might take place at any time.

The original meaning of the parable is quite clear. A number of details in the story represent the actual historical situation of the Jewish nation. The householder who planted the vineyard is God; the vineyard is the Jewish nation; the husbandmen who were placed over the vineyard are the priests and elders of the people; the servants that were sent again and again are the prophets of the Old Testament; the son who was cast out of the vineyard and killed is Jesus Christ himself. Thus the parable is a commentary on God's gracious dealings with his people, his constant pleadings for them to repent, their determination to persist in wickedness, their willingness even to kill Jesus, and their final and irrevocable rejection by God. Jesus asked his

---

[1]See Alfred Edersheim, *The Life and Times of Jesus the Messiah,* II, p. 423.

hearers what the owner of the vineyard would do to his rebellious servants. The Jews gave a ready response: "He will put those wretches to a miserable death, and let out the vineyard to other tenants who will give him the fruits in their season." Thus speaking, they unwittingly pronounced judgment against themselves.

Lessons from the Parable

Too often this parable is read as though nothing is to be seen in it except the doom of the Israelite nation. Certainly this is the main point that Jesus had in mind. When viewed from another standpoint, however, the parable assumes a slightly different character with certain definite lessons.

1. *It teaches us something about Christ.* In the parable Jesus is the son who was sent as the last opportunity for the evil tenants. According to Mark's account, Jesus represents himself as "a beloved son" and one who is "heir" of "the inheritance" (Mark 12:6-7). As Son he holds a unique place. The other messengers had come as servants. He came not as a servant but as the Beloved Son. Thus Jesus definitely sets himself apart from other men. His claims here and throughout his ministry were quite extraordinary. He said that he was the Bread of Life (John 6:35), the Light of the world (John 8:12), the Way, the Truth, and the Life (John 14:6). He came, he said, that men might have abundant life (John 10:10). He spoke of himself as being greater than Jonah and greater than Solomon (Matthew 12:41, 42). He existed before Abraham (John 8:58), and even before the world was created (John 17:5). He maintained that he and the Father are one (John 10:30), and, therefore, he said that to see him was to see the Father (John 14:9). These are stupendous claims, made by him who is known as the meekest and humblest of men; made without explanation or apology; stated by him as self-evident truths. These claims cannot easily be written off. They are a part of him, they explain him. Without them the whole personality of Jesus is submerged in an eternal enigma. Jesus claimed to be divine, and this parable is one of those passages that sets forth his claim in the clearest possible light.

2. *It teaches us something about men.* In the parable the vineyard planted by the householder had every possible advantage

— a hedge, a wine press, a tower, everything that was desirable. In the same way God had made ample provisions for Israel. He brought them out of Egypt and planted them in a good land. He took them to himself, gave them a written law, and they became his people. He lavished upon them his special concern and surrounded them with his special privileges. Yet Israel, the choice among the nations, utterly failed God and did not take advantage of its select position.

One lesson of the parable is that human privileges and human responsibilities cannot be taken lightly. When God makes provision for man, he expects something in return. This is the way it has always been. When times are good as they are now, when human freedoms are many, when the opportunities of living in a great land are so unlimited, God surely expects much of us. In the church our resources of wealth and learning have never been more abundant. Our opportunities to serve mankind and to reach the world with Christ's message have never been so vast. And these opportunities, numerous as they are, transmit to us certain inescapable responsibilities. There is an old legend that tells of how Jesus was received in heaven after his death and resurrection. One of the angels met him and said, "You must have suffered terribly for men down in the world." Jesus answered, "I did." "But do all men know," said the angel, "how much you loved them and suffered for them?" "No," said Jesus, "only a few men in the land of Palestine know about it." "What have you done," asked the angel, "to let other people know about it?" Jesus answered, "I have told Peter and James and John to tell others, and the others to tell the others, until all men know the story of how much I love them." On hearing this the angel was doubtful. "But what will happen," he said, "if Peter and James and John forget? What if they fail to tell the others? What then?" Back came the response of Jesus, "I haven't made any other plans; I'm counting on them." Peter, James, and John had received privileges that no one else had received; they had seen things that no other man had seen; and Jesus was counting on them. Their awesome responsibility has been handed down to us; and with our many advantages and abilities, Christ is surely counting on us.

3. *It teaches us something about God.* In the parable God is the patient householder who is looking for fruit from the vineyard. He sends the first messengers and they are cruelly rejected. He

waits. He sends other messengers, and they are likewise rejected. Still he waits. He tries to convict the evil tenants and restore in them a sense of honor. Finally he sends again. God is infinitely merciful and patient with men today. We may wonder sometimes why God is so patient with us. We sin often, we neglect our duties, we fail him in countless ways. We sometimes think that if we were in charge, we would have brought the world to an end long ago. But God's judgment delays. He does not want a single one to be lost (2 Peter 3:9). He is like the householder who, after continual rejection, sends his beloved Son in the hope that men will revere him.

The Greatest Sin

No truth in the Bible, however, is more plain than this: the patience of God can be exhausted with men. There is a limit even to divine grace. In the parable, after the wicked men had killed the Son, no more mercy could be shown. They had filled up the measure of their guilt.

The Jews committed the greatest of sins by rejecting Christ. They had been wayward and stubborn and fruitless for centuries; but their most atrocious crime was to take him who is Life and nail him to a cross. To reject Christ today is still to bring condemnation on oneself. "He who does not believe is condemned already, because he has not believed in the name of the only Son of God" (John 3:18). No man can remain neutral on Christ. Every man to whom the gospel is preached must either believe and follow him or commit sin by rejecting him. Luke's account of the parable, speaking of Christ as the stone, concludes with the statement: "Every one who falls on that stone will be broken to pieces; but when it falls on any one it will crush him" (Luke 20:18).

Discussion

1. Describe briefly the background that leads up to this parable. In what ways does this parable describe the historical situation of the Jewish nation?

2. Using the Four Gospels as a basis, how many Scriptures can you locate that give extraordinary claims of Jesus? What do these claims mean? How is Jesus making an unusual claim about himself in this parable?

3. It has been said that "human privileges and human responsibilities cannot be taken lightly." Discuss and illustrate this statement by reference to other passages of Scripture.

4. What evidences are there that God has been infinitely patient in his dealings with men? Discuss this in the light of his severity.

THE PARABLE OF THE TEN VIRGINS

" 'Then the kingdom of heaven shall be compared to ten maidens who took their lamps and went to meet the bridegroom. Five of them were foolish, and five were wise. For when the foolish took their lamps, they took no oil with them; but the wise took flasks of oil with their lamps. As the bridegroom was delayed, they all slumbered and slept. But at midnight there was a cry, "Behold, the bridegroom! Come out to meet him." Then all those maidens rose and trimmed their lamps. And the foolish said to the wise, "Give us some of your oil, for our lamps are going out." But the wise replied, "Perhaps there will not be enough for us and for you; go rather to the dealers and buy for yourselves." And while they went to buy, the bridegroom came, and those who were ready went in with him to the marriage feast; and the door was shut. Afterward the other maidens came also, saying, "Lord, lord, open to us." But he replied, "Truly, I say to you, I do not know you." Watch therefore, for you know neither the day nor the hour.' "

(Matthew 25:1-13)

Lesson 11

"THOSE WHO WERE READY"

Chapter 25 of Matthew presents a series of parables on preparedness: the parable of the Ten Virgins (vss. 1-13), the Parable of the Talents (vss. 14-30), and the Parable of the Sheep and the Goats (vss. 31-46). The series is an outgrowth of Jesus' discourse to his disciples on the fall of the city of Jerusalem and the time of his second coming (Matthew 24:3ff.). As he spoke of his second advent, Jesus warned that the time would arrive unexpectedly and would find many unprepared. He spoke of faithful and wise servants who did their duty while the master was away. He also spoke of evil servants who, thinking that the master was delayed, were careless and positively wicked in their conduct; and he said that when the master came, he would punish them in the place where "men will weep and gnash their teeth" (Matthew 24:45-51). Immediately following is the statement: "Then the kingdom of heaven shall be compared to ten maidens...." "Then" refers to the great event of the Lord's return. At that time the kingdom will be like the five wise and the five foolish virgins.

The Marriage Feast

Among the Jews the marriage of a boy and girl was looked upon as a matter that affected the entire family. The decision as to whom a son or daughter might marry was made by the parents or guardians. The arrangements were often agreed upon when the couple were still children. As the proposed marriage neared, a formal betrothal ceremony was held. At this time a dowry was paid to the parents of the bride. The transaction was regarded as final and the betrothal was absolutely binding. If for any reason the marriage did not take place, the girl could not be married to another unless she obtained a legal divorce. The betrothed couple was looked upon as husband and wife, and unfaithfulness on the part of either was considered adultery (Deuteronomy 22:23; Matthew 1:19). Following the betrothal, there was an interval of several months (or a year or so) before the marriage was consummated. What the marriage ceremony consisted of is not known. At the time of the wedding, which usually took place at night, a procession of some sort was held. Generally the friends of the bridegroom went and brought the bride and her attendants to the house of the groom. In the parable, however, the bridegroom is away from home. He is coming from a distance, and no one knows the exact time of his arrival. The maidens in the parable have gathered presumably in the bridal house and are waiting to go out and escort the bridegroom in. They have brought along with them their lamps. The lamps were made of pottery, shaped like a circular, covered bowl. On the side of each lamp a loop-like handle was affixed; at another point on the side there was a small opening where the wick was placed; and on the top was another opening to receive the oil. The kind of oil used in Palestine was the oil taken from the olive tree. The ordinary size lamp was small, so a wise person would supply himself with an adequate amount of oil. Failing to do this, five of the maidens in the parable were marked as foolish. While they were away trying to remedy their mistake, the bridegroom came, the marriage feast began, and the door was shut.

Certain points stand out clearly in the parable. The bridegroom who comes from a distance is Christ; the occasion of his coming is the joyous marriage feast; the time of his coming is unexpected, at midnight when people are heavy with sleep; the maidens who are waiting to go out and meet him are his professed disciples. The bride is not mentioned because she is not essential to the main theme of the parable.

What Cannot Be Done

Jesus' original audience for this story was his own disciples. It was given as a warning to his own followers, to those who had named his name and considered themselves a part of his own group. Dangers threaten the good as well as the godless. To his disciples, therefore, Jesus gives in this parable certain definite warnings. There are certain things that his disciples cannot afford to do.

1. *We cannot neglect preparation and be ready at his coming.* The foremost lesson of the parable is stated in these words: "Watch therefore, for you know neither the day nor the hour." The key word is "watch." What does this mean? How are Christians to watch for their Lord's return? It certainly does not mean that they must constantly fix their gaze on the sky, waiting for the first glimpse of his glorious appearance. It does not mean that they must talk of nothing else but his coming. Christians must watch with more than their eyes and their tongues. To watch is to have some forethought for the future, to take some prior precaution, to make some preliminary preparation; and it is to continue in that preparation always. This was the very thing that the foolish maidens failed to do. They had their lamps. They brought their oil. They began to wait eagerly. But they did not have enough oil. It never entered their minds that the bridegroom might be delayed. And because of this they were "foolish." They were not ungodly or immoral. They were not hypocrites. They were simply foolish. They did not allow for the possibility of delay; and when the lord finally came, they were unprepared.

One of the most inescapable lessons of life is the necessity of being prepared. Practically everything that is done requires preparation beforehand. It is true of reading, writing, and arithmetic; of buying and selling; of sowing and reaping; of winning and keeping friends. There are certain things in life which, if done at all, cannot be done at the last moment. Preparation is essential, for example, to knowledge. Every classroom teacher knows how big a problem it is to get students to give careful attention to their studies even when no special assignment is required. If only students worked as hard throughout the school year as they do the last night before a paper is due or the last hour before the final examination! The typical college classroom, before the bell rings, is filled with laughter and smiles and light-hearted conversation. As the teacher walks down the hall, he can hear the noise of the class. When he enters the room, scarcely a book is open. It is that way day after day — except the day of the final examination. On that day when it is too late, unless there has been previous study, then all is quiet, and every head is in a book. But the time of examination is not the time of preparation. No course of study can be mastered on the last night; and if the student is able to press into his brain enough facts to pass the examination, he will not be able to make use of them later when he needs them most.

This principle can be illustrated in other ways. Much preparation is required, for instance, before one takes a trip. If a person is going to travel around the world, he cannot wait until the last minute to get things ready. Many arrangements will have to be made at his business; at home a hundred and one little things must be attended to; all the minutiae to obtain a passport must be complied with; flight reservations and hotel reservations must be secured; sightseeing and excursion trips must be planned. And all of these things cannot be done on the last day. So if preparations need to be made before the time of an examination or before a long journey, surely it is necessary to make preparations for the greatest journey and the greatest examination of all: the journey into the Unseen World and the Final Examination before the Judge of the earth. On the day that Christ returns again, it will be too late to make up for the neglect of previous preparation. Christ will come at an unexpected time; and those are foolish who think that they will be able to buy their oil in the last hour after the shops have closed. The point of this parable is that Christians must be on constant watch for their Lord.

2. *We cannot borrow what must be bought.* Often when we read this parable we are ready to sympathize with the foolish maidens. Why did not the wise give to the foolish? How could they be so stingy and heartless and refuse to share their oil with others in the time of distress? The answer is: there are some things that must be bought; they cannot be borrowed. Character is like that. It cannot be loaned from person to person. Character is something that must be developed individually, resulting from God's working in one's life. A great man died the other day. He had lived long and well. Through the years he had planted his roots deep in the soil of proper conduct. He had become a veritable moral force for right. What a pity that his strength of will and his love of goodness could not be transferred to those who were at his bedside. But character cannot be bequeathed. Obedience to God is another thing that cannot be borrowed. Here each one is accountable individually. The husband cannot stand for the wife, nor the wife for the husband. All the faith and dedication in the world of parents is not enough for the children; and all the hope and enthusiasm of a

boy or girl cannot suffice for an indifferent father or mother. The plain truth is that God expects personal submission to his commands because he holds every man personally accountable for sins for which he has not received forgiveness. The Apostle Paul declares: "For we must all appear before the judgment seat of Christ, so that each one may receive good or evil, according to what he has done in the body" (2 Corinthians 5:10). In that day when men shall stand before Christ, it will be utterly impossible to slip into some empty life all those Christ-like qualities — faith, endurance, courage, obedience, and character. If these qualities are not individually gained in life, in the here and now, they cannot be imparted in the last hour of desperation. "So each of us shall give account of himself to God" (Romans 14:12).

3. *We cannot recall lost opportunities.* When the bridegroom came, the foolish maidens were out buying oil for their lamps. On returning, they found that the marriage feast had already begun. They missed their one chance. They did not seize their one great opportunity. Every day brings us opportunities that we must not neglect. Opportunities to help others abound around us. They are not only in Alaska and Nigeria. They are here, right at our hands.

> Seek not for fresher founts afar,
> Just drop your bucket where you are....
> Parch not your life with dry despair;
> The stream of hope flows everywhere —
> So under every sky and star,
> Just drop your bucket where you are.[1]

Today we may have before us an open door to do good. If we fail to go through that door, it will shut — shut us out from the joy of serving and shut us in with a selfish heart.

The pathetic truth of the parable is that the failure of the foolish maidens was final. The door was shut, and it was shut forever. How much those girls desired to enter! How long they had looked forward to the marriage of their friend! Yet they could not go in. Outside the banquet room, in the dark, they sob,

---

[1]Sam Walter Foss, *Opportunity.*

"Lord, lord, open to us." They were near to a welcomed reception, so near that they could hear the inexpressible joy inside, and yet so far. The exclusion was unalterably permanent.

Centuries later, long after the words of this parable have died out, the question still arises, "When will Christ come again?" That is the wrong question. The moment we think "when" we are in trouble. What should we be concerned about? Only whether or not our lamps are trimmed and burning! The one sure way to be ready on that day is to be ready every day.

Discussion

1. Make a list of parables that deal with the Second Coming of Christ.

2. Read the following passages of Scripture: John 14:1-3; Acts 1:9-11; Colossians 3:1-4: 1 Thessalonians 4:13-18; Hebrews 9:27,28; 2 Peter 3:1-10; Revelation 22:12-21. Many people today doubt that Jesus will come again. Is his Second Coming a matter of great importance? In what ways is it important? Have we minimized this in our preaching, our teaching, and in our daily conversation?

3. Tell something about a Jewish marriage feast. How is a marriage feast an appropriate figure to use in teaching on Christ's kingdom?

4. Discuss and illustrate the necessity of preparation for Christ's return.

5. Were the wise maidens selfish?

6. What does this parable teach on opportunities?

THE PARABLE OF THE TALENTS

" 'For it will be as when a man going on a journey called his servants and entrusted to them his property; to one he gave five talents, to another two, to another one, to each according to his ability. Then he went away. He who had received the five talents went at once and traded with them; and he made five talents more. So also, he who had the two talents made two talents more. But he who had received the one talent went and dug in the ground and hid his master's money. Now after a long time the master of those servants came and settled accounts with them. And he who had received the five talents came forward, bringing five talents more, saying, "Master, you delivered to me five talents; here I have made five talents more." His master said to him, "Well done, good and faithful servant; you have been faithful over a little, I will set you over much; enter into the joy of your master." And he also who had the two talents came forward, saying, "Master, you delivered to me two talents; here I have made two talents more." His master said to him, "Well done, good and faithful servant; you have been faithful over a little, I will set you over much; enter into the joy of your master." He also who had received the one talent came forward, saying, "Master, I knew you to be a hard man, reaping where you did not sow, and gathering where you did not winnow; so I was afraid, and I went and hid your talent in the ground. Here you have what is yours." But his master answered him, "You wicked and slothful servant! You knew that I reap where I have not sowed, and gather where I have not winnowed? Then you ought to have invested my money with the bankers, and at my coming I should have received what was my own with interest. So take the talent from him, and give it to him who has the ten talents. For to every one who has will more be given, and he will have abundance; but from him who has not, even what he has will be taken away. And cast the worthless servant into the outer darkness; there men will weep and gnash their teeth.' "

(Matthew 25:14-30)
(Similar Passage: Parable of the Pounds,
Luke 19:11-27)

Lesson 12

FAITHFUL SERVICE

The Parable of the Talents in Matthew and the Parable of the Pounds in Luke are in many ways quite similar. Each parable tells about a man who journeys to a far country; in each certain amounts of money are given to the servants, for which they are individually responsible; in each the lord, on his return, calls his servants in to settle accounts; in each there are those who have done well and are commended for their service; in each there is one man who, because he was afraid, utterly failed in his duty; and each parable concludes with the statement that the man who has will receive more, and from the man who has not will be taken away even what he has. For these reasons, some commentators maintain that what we have here are two versions of one original parable. But others affirm that the parables are independent of each other. For one thing, the circumstances of the parables are entirely different. According to Luke, Jesus told the story of the pounds "because he was near to Jerusalem, and because they supposed that the kingdom of God was to appear immediately" (Luke 19:11). In Matthew, however, Jesus speaks of the talents as he sits on the Mount of Olives (Matthew 24:3ff.), and this on the third day after his entry into Jerusalem. In Luke Jesus addresses publicly a mixed group that followed him, in Matthew Jesus talks privately with his disciples. The details of the two parables are likewise quite different. Alfred Plummer, in his learned commentary on Luke, has summarized these differences as follows: "(1) In the Talents we have a householder leaving home for a time, in the Pounds a nobleman going in quest of a crown; (2) the Talents are unequally distributed, the Pounds equally; (3) the sums entrusted differ enormously in amount; (4) in the Talents the rewards are the same, in the Pounds they differ and are proportionate to what has been gained; (5) in the Talents the unprofitable servant is severely punished, in the Pounds he is merely deprived of his pound. Out of about 302 words in Matthew and 286 in Luke, only about 66 words or parts of words are common to the two."[1] And then Plummer adds: "An estimate of the probabilities on each side seems to be favourable to the view that we have accurate reports of two different parables, and not two reports of the same parable...."[2]

Distinct as it is from the Parable of the Pounds, the Parable of the Talents serves as a perfect complement to the Parable of the Ten Virgins. In the preceding story the maidens are pictured as waiting for their lord; in this story the servants are represented as working for their lord. One stresses the duty of constant alertness, the other the duty of faithful service. Put together both teach the Christian that as he watches he must not be idle, that the best way to be ready is to be busy in the Master's business.

The Entrusted Talents

As Jesus' story goes, before the master left home to go to another country, he called all of his servants in and gave each of them a definite sum of money. The amount of money put in their care varied, depending on the ability of the servants, but in each case the kind of money involved was the talent. The talent in Biblical times was no small sum. Originally it was not a coin but a measurement of weight, equal to about seventy-five pounds. In the time of Jesus one talent was worth nearly a thousand dollars. The servants in the story were actually slaves, the owner's property as much as the money placed in their charge. On returning from his journey, the master called his servants in. Obviously he expected them to put his money to good use while he was away, and this they understood. The first two servants had done well, for they had doubled the amounts given them. The third servant, putting off seeing his master to the last, turned his money back without any increase. His excuse was that he knew his master was a hard man, and so fearing that he would displease him, he slipped out and buried his gift in the ground. The servants who did well were praised, but the

[1]Alfred Plummer, *A Critical and Exegetical Commentary on the Gospel According to St. Luke*, p. 437.
[2]*Ibid.*

servant who failed was excluded from further service and was flung into the outer darkness.

Lessons From the Talents

Some interpreters see the unprofitable servant in this parable as the main character of the story. They maintain, therefore, that the unprofitable servant represents the scribes and Pharisees and the other Jews who would not run the risk of giving full-fledged allegiance to Christ. Possibly there is some merit to this interpretation. But it must be remembered that when this parable was spoken, none of the outside Jews were present, that Jesus' intimate disciples were his sole audience. The primary application of the parable, then, must be to the disciples rather than to the Jews at large.

The lessons of the talents focus attention upon three scenes.

1. *The gifts.* The parable opens with a description of the distribution of gifts: "For it will be as when a man going on a journey called his servants and entrusted to them his property; to one he gave five talents, to another two, to another one, to each according to his ability." The first thing that strikes us here is that each man received something. Not a single servant was passed over, no one left the master's chamber with empty pockets. This is true of all of us. No person responsible to God is left out in the divine distribution of gifts. Each person receives something. Indeed, each person receives much. Even the one talent servant received the large sum of a thousand dollars. So God has a work for every man, and God gives to every man enough capital to accomplish the work that he intends for him to do.

But each servant, though he received something, did not receive the same gift. To one was given five talents, to another two, and to another one. Each man was given an amount in keeping with his ability. That is the way God acts. He does not expect of us what we cannot do. Our native abilities differ. Some of us are born with strong and active bodies, while others enter the world in poor health, with inherited susceptibility to certain diseases. A few are gifted with superior intellects, many others with something less. Also, our opportunities to develop our gifts differ. A boy brought up in the outdoors is more likely to attain to his physical maximum than a boy restricted to the neighborhood of a big city. In spiritual matters, young men and young women in a small congregation often grow rapidly to Christian leadership, where in a large congregation they may fail to grow because they feel that they are not needed. And even after our gifts have been developed, our opportunities to use them may not be the same. Now there are, of course, always opportunities to serve, but for some the opportunities may not be as many as for others. Not all fields at one moment are glowing with a golden harvest. There are some fields where the ground needs to be prepared; there are other fields that are waiting for the sowing; and, to be sure, not all fields when sown are capable of producing the same crop. So our opportunities, like our innate endowments, vary from person to person. These comprise the "talents" which the Lord gives us. The talents are not just our natural abilities, for the talents are given to each individual according to his ability. All of what God gives to men to perform his tasks are included in the talents.

2. *The use of the gifts.* What was the result of the master's confidence in his servants? To what use did they put his money while he was away? The servants who received the larger sums immediately went to work. They invested their money in profitable enterprises and succeeded in doubling their fortunes. We are not to think that such eminent success came to them without trial. How many must have been the times that they thought of recklessly spending their master's money, or that they teased with the idea of sitting back and playing it safe? Temptations come to the five talent man as well as to the one talent man. Nor are we to think that the success of these servants was due to an unusual run of luck. Only for one reason were they successful, and that because of hard work.

While two of the servants attained greatness, the other servant followed a path that ended in bleak failure. Why did he fail? Why did he bring shame upon himself and disappoint his master? It was not that he purposed to fail. He doubtless left his master's presence with the firm intention to justify the confidence that had been placed in him. Nevertheless, he failed. There are several reasons for his failure. First, he failed because he did not have faith in himself. He was unsure of his own abilities. When he compared his gift with the larger gifts, he was afraid that he could not do as much as his fellow servants. Not wanting to do the least, he decided to do nothing. Some people are that way. If they cannot have the leading part, they want no part at all; if they are not able to do some really big thing, and gain the approval of their fellows, they will do nothing at all. Sometimes churches that are small make the mistake of thinking that because they cannot support many missionaries abroad, they cannot support at least one. Yet each congregation, no matter what its size, has some responsibility in reaching out to a lost world. How many times we, like the one talent man, fail without giving it a try!

Second, this man failed because he did not have courage to work. His master called him a slothful servant. He was afraid of work. Again and again we see that this is the cause of most failures in life. If a man does not work, if he is not willing to pay the price in hard labor, he will never be crowned with success. The same holds true with spiritual things. God has bestowed his grace upon us, but we can multiply our talents in his service only by work.

Third, he failed because he did not have faith in his master. He thought that he would get a bad deal. He pictured his lord as a hard man. Some people look upon God in the same way. Some conceive of God as a stern Power that either is making unreasonable demands or is pushing people around to get his own way. If this is so, if God is like an exacting taskmaster that never lets up, this is all the more reason why we should strive to use the talents he has given us. But, of course, this view of God is utterly untrue. He does not simply order and demand. He loves and pities and extends his arms in mercy. When he gives us a task, he gives us the means to accomplish the task; and he never requires of us something without giving us the power to do it.

3. *The consequences of using and not using.* The parable tells what happened when the master returned home. There was a time of reckoning. Each servant was summoned in to account for his conduct. The man who had received five talents had gained five more. "Well done, good and faithful servant," says the master. The two talent man had gained two other talents. His master said to him, "Well done, good and faithful servant." In each case the words of commendation were precisely the

same. The master was equally pleased with the service of both. And for them there was a twofold reward. The first was that they would be given even more than they had. "You have been faithful over a little, I will set you over much.... For to every one who has will more be given, and he will have abundance." The second reward was that they were admitted into the joy of their lord. This meant that they were granted the right to sit at their lord's banquet table. It was a privilege that slaves never received and one which, perhaps, automatically gave them their freedom.

But the idle servant was forbidden to share the joy and honor at the master's table. And besides, all that he had was extracted from him. His one talent was put into the hands of the man with ten talents. Is that not evidence that his master was harsh? No; it is the inevitable consequence of doing nothing. It is a law of life that we lose what we fail to use. It may be that a person has some special ability. As he uses that ability day after day, his ability increases; if he does not use it, his efficiency in that thing will diminish to nothing. A new word, a new name, a new story not quickly repeated is soon forgotten. Any artistic skill or athletic dexterity requires constant sharpening. So in the spiritual realm every gift given by God must be put to work or else it will be taken from us.

What was the difference between the servants? Why were two profitable and one unprofitable? The answer lies not in the fact that the two from the beginning were more gifted. With all their ability they still could have been lazy and buried their talents. It was not because they were brilliant or because they had a knack for business that they were commended. They were commended simply because they had been faithful in the service of their absent lord. Each man, with the ability that he possessed, had done his best. When we, too, turn to the Eternal Home, it may be that some will come with arms full of trophies, and that others will come with not as many; but the Lord will meet us with the only words that count, "Well done, good and faithful servant."

Discussion

1. Compare and contrast the Parable of the Talents and the Parable of the Pounds. In your opinion, are these two independent parables or two versions of one parable?

2. What lessons are to be derived from the fact that the master gave talents to each of his servants? What is a talent? What do the talents represent?

3. Why did the one talent man fail? What was his view of the master? What was the master's view of him?

4. How is it that "we lose what we fail to use"? Is this true of spiritual matters as well as physical?

THE PARABLE OF THE SHEEP AND THE GOATS

" 'When the Son of man comes in his glory, and all the angels with him, then he will sit on his glorious throne. Before him will be gathered all the nations, and he will separate them one from another as a shepherd separates the sheep from the goats, and he will place the sheep at his right hand, but the goats at the left. Then the King will say to those at his right hand, "Come, O blessed of my Father, inherit the kingdom prepared for you from the foundation of the world; for I was hungry and you gave me food, I was thirsty and you gave me drink, I was a stranger and you welcomed me, I was naked and you clothed me, I was sick and you visited me, I was in prison and you came to me." Then the righteous will answer him, "Lord, when did we see thee hungry and feed thee, or thirsty and give thee drink? And when did we see thee a stranger and welcome thee, or naked and clothe thee? And when did we see thee sick or in prison and visit thee?" And the King will answer them, "Truly, I say to you, as you did it to one of the least of these my brethren, you did it to me." Then he will say to those at his left hand, "Depart from me, you cursed, into the eternal fire prepared for the devil and his angels; for I was hungry and you gave me no food, I was thirsty and you gave me no drink, I was a stranger and you did not welcome me, naked and you did not clothe me, sick and in prison and you did not visit me." Then they also will answer, "Lord, when did we see thee hungry or thirsty or a stranger or naked or sick or in prison, and did not minister to thee?" Then he will answer them, "Truly, I say to you, as you did it not to one of the least of these, you did it not to me." And they will go away into eternal punishment, but the righteous into eternal life.' "

(Matthew 25:31-46)

Lesson 13

IF ONLY WE HAD KNOWN

The two foregoing parables especially concern Christians, those who are waiting to go out to meet the Bridegroom and those who, while waiting, are engaged in the service of their Lord. This parable, however, envisions all men, for it tells of a final and irreversible judgment of the whole world. For this reason it is more than a parable: it is a realistic prediction of the future in which all nations are brought before the Son of man (see Revelation 20:12-13). Jesus himself is the Son of man, and in keeping with his father's wish he proceeds to judge the nations (see John 5:22,23; Acts 17:30,31). He makes division among them like a shepherd who separates the sheep from the goats. In Palestine the task of distinguishing between them was not difficult, for the sheep were white and the goats were black. He places the sheep at his right hand, the position of distinction and honor (1 Kings 2:19; Acts 2:33,34). The goats he turns aside and puts on his left hand. Then the awards are announced. To the righteous the Son says, "Come, inherit the kingdom prepared for you from the foundation of the world." All their lives they had lived in sympathy and self-sacrifice. Now the kingdom that was theirs in God's eternal purpose was to be theirs in actual possession. But the very characteristics that won for them the King's approval were the same characteristics, when absent, that caused the others to be rejected. Those on the left hand had shown no pity and had practiced no self-denial. The kingdom prepared for them was not to be theirs, nothing was to be theirs except eternal punishment ready for the devil and his angels.

Giving to Others

This parable has through the centuries been interwoven into the basic texture of Christianity. How often a Christian is defined in the very terms of this passage, a person who visits the sick, clothes the needy, gives food to the hungry and offers drink to the thirsty. The reason why these things are so often remembered is because Jesus made them in this scene the standard of judgment for right conduct, the final proof as to whether a man is really his disciple. In that Day it will not be a question of how much we know, what creed we can recite, or how many theological definitions we can unravel. It will not even be how good we have been in our morals and ethics. But it will be a question of how much good we have done, a question of how well our deepest feelings have been expressed by the positive action of giving to others. One of the famous preachers of the past explicitly made it known to his congregation that when the gifts to the poor were no longer sufficient, the sacred vessels of the church would be melted down to supply the deficiency. The really important thing, according to Jesus, is how we have responded to the needs of our brothers.

Giving in Simple Things

There are countless lessons in this parable. Jesus here not only enforces the principle of giving, but he puts the principle within the reach of all. In every case we see that the help given was a simple thing. Many times we ask ourselves, "What can I do to help others?" And we conclude, because we are not trained to be missionaries, because we cannot give thousands of dollars to send others to go, that what we can do is too little and therefore we do nothing. Yet what the righteous did in this parable is what every man can do. How important is one act of unexpected kindness, one call to a newcomer in town, one word of invitation to a man who does not know Christ! William Barclay retells a story told by Alexander Whyte, the famous preacher of Edinburgh.[1] A business man by the name of Rigby used to stop regularly at Edinburgh. Rigby was by no means a preacher; he could hardly talk to anyone about religion. But one thing he did: each Sunday when he was in Edinburgh he went to church, and each Sunday he did his best to bring someone with him. One day he invited a young man to go with him. The man stubbornly refused, but Rigby insisted and finally the young man agreed to

---

[1]William Barclay, *And Jesus Said: A Handbook on the Parables of Jesus*, p. 121.

go. As a result of the morning service, the young man wanted to attend again in the evening. And that night he decided to give himself to Christ. The next morning Rigby passed by Whyte's house. He had never met Whyte, but on a sudden impulse he decided to stop and get acquainted with him. Rigby told him about the young man; and Whyte was glad to hear it because he felt that his sermon the night before had fallen flat." What did you say your name was?" Whyte asked. "Rigby," said the man. "Man," said Whyte, "You're the man I've been looking for for years." He then turned and went back to his study and brought out a bundle of letters. All of the letters were the same, telling of how a man by the name of Rigby had invited them to church, and of how as a result, their whole lives had been changed. Whyte told Rigby that twelve of the letters were from young men, and that four of them had already entered the ministry. It was not a large thing that Rigby did, but with the blessing of God his efforts brought much fruit.

Giving Without Reward

We note in this parable also that those who had done so many good deeds were quite unaware of their goodness. They had performed their acts of love and mercy unsolicited. Their kindness was spontaneous. And they were greatly surprised at the end when the King so richly rewarded them. That is the way giving should always be, unasked and unconcerned about praise. Jesus was constantly emphasizing this point. There were the Pharisees who gave for the glory of themselves. They practiced their piety in order to be seen by men (Matt. 6:1).[2] Thus Jesus declared that they had all the reward they were going to get. The Greek verb here is *apecho*. In New Testament times it was a very familiar term. It was the ordinary word that was used on a receipt, to show that a debt had been paid in full.[3] So Jesus says that those who give to honor themselves receive their full payment in human praise. They gain no other reward.

---

[2]The Greek construction *pros to theathenai* is every emphatic, an articular infinitive of purpose. This is translated very well in the Revised Standard Version.

[3]See Arndt-Gingrich, *A Greek English Lexicon of the New Testament and Other Early Christian Literature.* 2nd ed., p. 84f. Paul's statement "I have received full payment" (Philippians 4:18, Revised Standard Version) is an excellent rendering of *apecho*.

Our giving today must be such that the left hand does not know what the right hand is doing (Matt. 6:3). This statement of Jesus can be misunderstood. It does not teach "secret giving," as though it is necessary to slip our gifts into the collection plate while no one is looking on. For the right hand to give without the left hand knowing it, refers to our motives in giving. That is to say, the right hand should give so unpretentiously, with so little desire for credit, that the left hand does not even know what it is doing. There is a beautiful story of an old saint who was offered anything he desired because he had done so many good deeds. His only request was that he might be granted the ability to do good without knowing that he was doing good. And so it happened that wherever he went his shadow cast a blessing after him. The righteous in the parable had done good, but they scarcely remembered it.

Giving to Christ

But the most remarkable thing in this parable is that the people who gave so generously did not know that they were really giving to Christ. They say, "Lord, when did we see you hungry or thirsty or naked? When did we see you ill or in prison? When we did those deeds, when we gave food to that starving man, when we took that stranger in, when we took care of that sick person through the night, we didn't know that was you." "Inasmuch," says Jesus, "that you did it to the least of my brothers, you did it to me." What a startling revelation it was for them to learn that they had actually ministered to Christ.

This parable poses a situation that every person needs to contemplate: "Suppose Christ was on earth today. What would be my attitude toward him. How much would I be concerned about him? What kind of treatment would I give him?" We are ready to answer, being quite liberal with ourselves, that we would be very much interested in him. We would not neglect him. Certainly we would not mistreat him. But, of course, Christ is not here today in flesh and blood. However, and this is a matter that we too often forget, his brothers are here, and whatever we do for them we do for him. We may think of it like this. God, the Almighty One, does not need any one of us. Because he is God, he does not need a single thing that we might give him. Yet God is also a Father, and all men are his children. And the God who in one sense we can do nothing for, in another sense we can do everything for by loving and providing for his children. The only way that we can do anything for God is to do something for his children.

On the other hand, what will God's attitude be toward us if we fail to help his children? Clearly, if we fail them we fail him. This was the very thing that those who were rejected could not understand. They say, "Lord, when did we see you hungry or thirsty or ill or in prison? When did we see you on the streets begging? If we had known that it was you in trouble, we would have helped you!" We are the same today. We often discriminate in our giving. We do not mind helping some dear friend or associate or well-known brother, someone who is our social equal who happens to be overtaken by misfortune. Perhaps we do not mind giving a meal every now and then to an honest-looking beggar. But to be willing to aid everyone, to treat every person with the same concern and respect that we would have for the Lord himself, is something that we have not as yet realized in our lives.

It is sad to think that there was a time in the history of earth when men rejected Christ. We find it hard to believe that such a rejection ever occurred. If only we had seen him as he walked the worn paths of Palestine; if we had heard those words of soft exhortation by Galilee's Sea; if we had witnessed his signs and seen his glory; if we had lived in his time and in his country — no, we would not have denied him or turned him away, we would not have marched him to a cross! But it does not help to say what we would have done had we been there. Jesus came to men then, but he still comes today, to your city and to mine. How do we treat him? Do we welcome him? G. A. Studdert-Kennedy of Birmingham, England, wrote:

> When Jesus came to Golgotha, they
>   hanged him on a tree;
> They drove great nails through hands
>   and feet and made a Calvary;
> They crowned him with a crown of thorns,
>   red were his wounds and deep;
> For those were crude and cruel days,
>   and human flesh was cheap.

When Jesus came to Birmingham, they
    simply passed him by;
They never hurt a hair of him,
    they only let him die;
For men had grown more tender,
    they would not give him pain;
They only passed on down the street,
    and left him in the rain.

Still Jesus cried, "Forgive them
    for they know not what they do."
And still it rained the winter rain
    and drenched him through and through;
The crowds went home and left the street
    without a soul to see;
Jesus crouched against a wall
    and cried for Calvary!

And in the Final Day the lamemt of many will be the lament
expressed in the parable, "Lord, we didn't know that it was
you!"

Discussion

1. In what sense is this picture of judgment not a parable? In what sense is it
   a parable?

2. What is the main lesson of this story?

3. Jesus teaches here the importance of little things. What other Scriptures
   teach the same lesson? Why are little things so important?

4. What quality does Christ possess which enables him to be identified with
   the person in need?